S0-AFC-907

Reading EXPLORER 2

Paul MacIntyre

HEINLE
CENGAGE Learning™

Australia • Brazil • Japan • Korea • Mexico • Singapore • Spain • United Kingdom • United States

HEINLE
CENGAGE Learning

Reading Explorer 2
Paul MacIntyre

VP and Director of Operations: Vincent Grosso
Publisher: Andrew Robinson
Editorial Manager: Sean Bermingham
Senior Development Editor: Derek Mackrell
Assistant Editor: Claire Tan
Technology Development Manager: Debie Mirtle
Technology Project Manager: Pam Prater
Asset Development Coordinator: Noah Vincelette
Director of Global Marketing: Ian Martin
Director of US Marketing: Jim McDonough
Content Project Manager: Tan Jin Hock
Senior Print Buyer: Mary Beth Hennebury
National Geographic Coordinator: Leila Hishmeh
Contributing Writers: Colleen Sheils, Sue Leather
Cover/Text Designer: Page 2, LLC
Compositor: Page 2, LLC
Cover Images: (Top) Raul Touzon/National Geographic Image Collection, (bottom) Tim Laman/ National Geographic Image Collection

Credits appear on pages 191–192, which constitutes a continuation of the copyright page.

Acknowledgments
The Author and Publishers would like to thank the following teaching professionals for their valuable feedback during the development of this series.

Jamie Ahn, English Coach, Seoul; **Heidi Bundschoks**, ITESM, Sinaloa México; **José Olavo de Amorim**, Colégio Bandeirantes, São Paulo; **Marina Gonzalez**, Instituto Universitario de Lenguas Modernas Pte., Buenos Aires; **Tsung-Yuan Hsiao**, National Taiwan Ocean University, Keelung; **Michael Johnson**, Muroran Institute of Technology; **Thays Ladosky**, Colégio Damas, Recife; **Ahmed Mohamed Motala**, University of Sharjah; **David Persey**, British Council, Bangkok; **David Schneer**, ACS International, Singapore; **Atsuko Takase**, Kinki University, Osaka; **Deborah E. Wilson**, American University of Sharjah

Additional thanks to Yulia P. Boyle, Jim Burch, Michael Colonna, and Dierdre Bevington-Attardi at National Geographic Society; and to Nancy Douglas for her helpful comments and suggestions.

This series is dedicated to the memory of Joe Dougherty, who was a constant inspiration throughout its development.

Copyright © 2009 Heinle, Cengage Learning

ALL RIGHTS RESERVED. No part of this work covered by the copyright herein may be reproduced, transmitted, stored, or used in any form or by any means graphic, electronic, or mechanical, including but not limited to photocopying, recording, scanning, digitizing, taping, Web distribution, information networks, or information storage and retrieval systems, except as permitted under Section 107 or 108 of the 1976 United States Copyright Act, without the prior written permission of the publisher.

For permission to use material from this text or product, submit all requests online at **www.cengage.com/permissions**
Further permissions questions can be emailed to
permissionrequest@cengage.com

Student Book ISBN-13: 978-1-4240-2934-1
Student Book ISBN-10: 1-4240-2934-1
Student Book + Student CD-ROM ISBN-13: 978-1-4240-2937-2
Student Book + Student CD-ROM ISBN-10: 1-4240-2937-6
Student Book (US edition) ISBN-13: 978-1-4240-4364-4
Student Book (US edition) ISBN-10: 1-4240-4364-6

Heinle
20 Channel Center
Boston, Massachusetts 02210
USA

Cengage Learning is a leading provider of customized learning solutions with office locations around the globe, including Singapore, the United Kingdom, Australia, Mexico, Brazil, and Japan. Locate our local office at:
international.cengage.com/region

Cengage Learning products are represented in Canada by Nelson Education, Ltd.

Visit Heinle online at **elt.heinle.com**
Visit our corporate website at **www.cengage.com**

Printed in Canada
2 3 4 5 6 7 – 12 11 10 09

☐ Contents

Explore Your World!   4
Scope and Sequence   6
Introduction   8

Unit 1 On the Menu   **9**
Unit 2 Animals and Language   **21**
Unit 3 History Detectives   **33**

Review Quiz   45
World Heritage Spotlight: Buried Cities   46
A Global View: Languages   48
Vocabulary Building   50

Unit 4 Great Destinations   **51**
Unit 5 Storms   **63**
Unit 6 Reef Encounters   **75**

Review Quiz   87
World Heritage Spotlight: Underwater Wonders   88
A Global View: Water   90
Vocabulary Building   92

Unit 7 Sweet Scents   **93**
Unit 8 Great Explorers   **105**
Unit 9 Traditions and Rituals   **117**

Review Quiz   129
World Heritage Spotlight: Cities of Gold and Mud   130
A Global View: Trade   132
Vocabulary Building   134

Unit 10 Global Warming   **135**
Unit 11 Incredible Insects   **147**
Unit 12 Going to Extremes   **159**

Review Quiz   171
World Heritage Spotlight: The Grand Canyon   172
A Global View: Climate   174
Vocabulary Building   176

Vocabulary Index   177
Video Scripts   179
Credits   191

Get ready to Explore Your World!

The world's longest mammal migration ends here in the **North Pacific**. Which animal holds the record? **p. 24**

In 2004, a private spaceship took off from a **California** desert on a journey to the edge of space. Whose spaceship was it? **p. 161**

One of the worst disasters in U.S. history occurred in **New Orleans** in 2005. What caused it? **p. 65**

NORTH AMERICA

Puerto Rico is famous for *sofrito*. What is it—and how do you make it? **p. 16**

In **Arizona**, visitors can cross a bridge that's more than a kilometer above the ground. Where is it? **p. 172**

Panama's *Eciton burchellii* is one of the world's most frightening creatures. What kind of animal is it? **p. 149**

SOUTH AMERICA

A rose can travel from a **Colombian** mountain to a U.S. flower store in just three days. How is it possible? **p. 96**

Chacaltaya in **Bolivia** was once the world's highest ski resort—but not any more. What happened to it? **p. 137**

The towns of **Pompeii and Herculaneum** were destroyed during two terrible days in 79 A.D. What happened? **p. 46**

The explorer Marco Polo spent 17 years traveling in **China**. What things amazed him the most? **p. 107**

The largest sumo wrestlers in **Japan** weigh more than 280kg. How do they get so big? **p. 119**

EUROPE

ASIA

AFRICA

In 2007, a 500-year-old love letter was discovered with the body of a **Korean** man. Who was the letter from? **p. 38**

Europeans once believed the city of **Timbuktu** was made of gold. Was this true—and what is it like today? **p. 130**

A train in **Darjeeling** takes ten hours to travel 80 kilometers. Why is it so slow? **p. 62**

AUSTRALIA

Great white sharks are found in the waters of **South Africa** and other places. Are they really fearless killers? **p. 82**

The largest structure made by living things can be found off the coast of **Queensland, Australia**. What is it—and how was it made? **p. 88**

ANTARCTICA

Scope and Sequence

Unit	Theme	Lesson	Reading Passage	Vocabulary Building	Video
1	On the Menu	**A:** The Home of the Olive **B:** A Taste of the Caribbean	An Oil for Life Sofrito Sensation	Word Partnership: *evidence* Usage: *contrast*	**Greek Olives**
2	Animals and Language	**A:** Ocean Giants **B:** Our Bond with Dogs	Song of the Humpback Dogs in a Human World	Usage: *alarm/harm* Thesaurus: *talent*	**Man's Best Friend**
3	History Detectives	**A:** Secrets of the Pharaohs **B:** A Body in the Mountains	Was King Tut Murdered? Who Killed the Iceman?	Word Link: *teen* Word Partnership: *debate*	**Inca Mummy**
Review 1	Buried Cities	**World Heritage Spotlight:** Pompeii and Herculaneum, Italy		**A Global View:** Languages Word Partnership: *language* Word Link: *–en/– ness*	
4	Great Destinations	**A:** Big City Travel **B:** Postcards from India	Grand Central Terminal Mumbai: City of Dreams	Word Partnership: *location* Word Partnership: *policy*	**Mountain Train**
5	Storms	**A:** When Disaster Strikes **B:** Superstorm	The Flooding of New Orleans Tropical Cyclones	Word Partnership: *neighborhood* Word Partnership: *qualify*	**Birth of a Hurricane**
6	Reef Encounters	**A:** Coral Reefs **B:** The Truth About Sharks	Cities Beneath the Sea Shark Attack!	Word Partnership: *negative* Word Link: *in–*	**Swimming with Sharks**
Review 2	Underwater Wonders	**World Heritage Spotlight:** Great Barrier Reef, Australia		**A Global View:** Water Word Link: *–(a)tion*	

Unit	Theme	Lesson	Reading Passage	Vocabulary Building	Video
7	Sweet Scents	**A:** The Business of Flowers **B:** Marketing Perfume	The Flower Trade Perfume: A Promise in a Bottle	Word Partnership: *handle* Word Partnership: *obtain*	**Madagascar Perfume**
8	Great Explorers	**A:** Marco Polo **B:** Prince of Travelers	Marco Polo in China The Travels of Ibn Battuta	Word Partnership: *undertake* Thesaurus: *remote*	**Crossing Antarctica**
9	Traditions and Rituals	**A:** A Sporting Ritual **B:** Marriage Traditions	Giants of the Ring Bride of the Sahara	Word Partnership: *impact* Word Link: *re–*	**Nubian Wedding**
Review 3	Cities of Gold and Mud	**World Heritage Spotlight:** Djénné and Timbuktu, Mali		**A Global View:** Trade Word Link: *–ism* Word Link: *inter–*	
10	Global Warming	**A:** A Warming World **B:** Arctic Survivors	The Big Thaw Last Days of the Ice Hunters	Word Partnership: *uncover* Usage: *I'm starving!*	**Global Warming**
11	Incredible Insects	**A:** Small Wonders **B:** Unexpected Beauty	Army Ants The Beauty of Moths	Word Link: *co–* Word Partnership: *disturb*	**Kenya Butterflies**
12	Going to Extremes	**A:** To the Edge of Space **B:** Dark Descent	Private Space Flight The Deepest Cave	Usage: *dozen* Word Partnership: *necessity*	**Young Adventurers**
Review 4	The Grand Canyon	**World Heritage Spotlight:** Grand Canyon National Park, U.S.A.		**A Global View:** Climate Word Link: *–ologist*	

Introduction

Welcome to Reading Explorer!

In this book, you'll travel the world, explore different cultures, and discover interesting topics. You'll also become a better reader!

Reading will be easier—and you'll understand more—if you ask yourself these questions:

What do I already know?

- Before you read, look at the photos, captions, and maps. Ask yourself: *What do I already know about this topic?*
- Think about the language you know—or may need to know— to understand the topic.

What do I want to learn?

- Look at the title and headings. Ask yourself: *What is this passage about? What will I learn?*
- As you read, check your predictions.

What have I learned?

- As you read, take notes. Use them to help you answer questions about the passage.
- Write down words you learn in a vocabulary notebook.

How can I learn more?

- Practice your reading skills and vocabulary in the Review Units.
- Explore the topics by watching the videos in class, or at home using the CD-ROM.

Now you're ready to explore your world!

heading   title   photo

map

caption

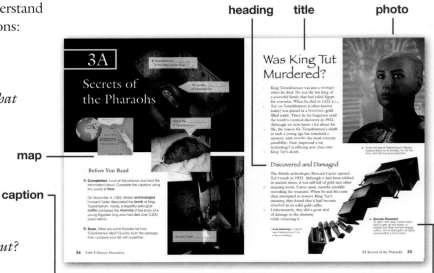

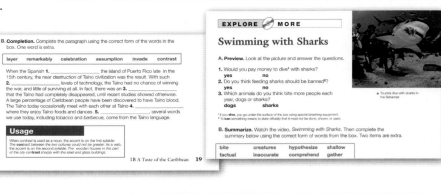

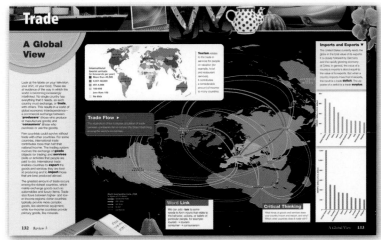

UNIT 1

On the Menu

Discuss these questions with a partner.

1. Do you like to try new foods?

2. Do you have a favorite foreign food?

3. What interesting dishes can you make?

▲ Student chefs use woks and open flames to prepare vegetables in Hefei, China.

9

1A The Home of the Olive

SPAIN

TUSCANY

•Madrid

ITALY

M E D I T E R R A N E A N   S E A

GREECE

TURKEY

SYRIA

TUNISIA

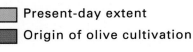

Present-day extent

Origin of olive cultivation

0 mi   500
0 km   500

NATIONAL GEOGRAPHIC MAPS

Before You Read

A. Completion. Look at the map and read the information below. Then complete the sentences below using the correct form of the words in **blue**.

The earliest olive **cultivation** occurred in the eastern Mediterranean about 6,000 years ago. Today, the world's largest **producers** of olive oil are still found around the Mediterranean Sea, where the strong heat and bright sun **enhance** the oil's flavor. The process of **harvesting** the olives, and **separating** the oil from the water and solids, has remained largely unchanged for thousands of years.

1. If you _____ things, you move them apart.
2. To _____ something means to improve its value, or quality.
3. If you _____ land, you prepare and grow crops on it.
4. When you _____ a crop, you gather it in.
5. If you _____ something, you make or create it.

B. Skim for the Main Idea. On the next page, look at the title, photos, and first paragraph. What is this reading mainly about?

a. how to cook using olive oil
b. the history and benefits of olive oil
c. some famous olive growers

An Oil for Life

1   Maria Alcalá of Madrid speaks for many Mediterranean people when she says that "a meal without olive oil would be a bore." No one knows when the Mediterranean civilizations initially fell in love with olives. That occurred before recorded history. However, there is

5   evidence that the cultivation of olive trees began in countries around the Mediterranean Sea in approximately 4000 B.C., and 2,000 years after that people in the eastern Mediterranean region began to produce oil from olives. The Mediterranean still accounts for 99 percent of all world olive oil production.

10 From ancient times until today, the basic process of producing the oil is the same. First, whole olives are crushed.[1] Then, the liquid is separated from the solids. After that, the valuable oil is separated from the water.

    Many olive growers maintain their ancient traditions
15 and still harvest the olives by hand. "We . . . harvest in the traditional way," says Don Celso, an olive farmer from Tuscany, Italy. "It would be less expensive to do it with machines, but it's
20 more a social thing. Twenty people come to help with the harvest, and we pay them in oil."

[1] When you **crush** something, you break it into pieces by applying pressure.

▲ Olive oil has been produced at this home in Tuscany, Italy, for nearly 1,000 years.

Leading olive oil producers
(% of world production)

Spain 36%   Italy 25%
                Greece 18%
                    Tunisia 8%
                        Turkey 5%
                            Syria 4%

▲ Rows of young olive trees line the hills of Andalusia in Spain, the world's leading olive oil producer.

The Benefits of Olive Oil

25 Olive oil has had a variety of uses through its long history. In ancient times, olive oil was used as money and as medicine. It was even used during war—heated up and dropped down on attackers. It is still used in religious ceremonies. It is great for protecting the freshness of fish and cheese. There are even olive oil lamps and olive oil soaps.[2]

30 One important study showed that Mediterranean people have the lowest rate of heart disease among Western nations. This is partly associated with their frequent use of olive oil. Other studies have shown that food cooked in olive oil is healthier, and that eating olive oil twice a day reduces women's risk of getting breast cancer.[3] The world is
35 beginning to understand its benefits, and olive oil is no longer an unusual sight at dinner tables outside the Mediterranean region. The olive oil producing countries now sell large amounts of olive oil to countries in Europe, Asia, Africa, and North and South America.

Olive oil enhances the lives of people
40 everywhere. Its benefits, recently confirmed by science, were already understood in ancient times. Mediterranean people are happy to share their secret with the world.

[2] **Soap** is a material used for cleaning the hands, the body, etc.

[3] **Cancer** is a serious disease in which cells in the body grow rapidly in an uncontrolled way.

A careful pouring of olive oil ▶ turns a plate of sheep cheese into a work of art.

Reading Comprehension

A. Multiple Choice. Choose the correct answer for each question.

Purpose

1. What is the purpose of this passage?
  a. to compare Mediterranean olive oil with that produced in other places
  b. to show why olive oil is produced around the Mediterranean Sea
  c. to discuss olive oil production outside the Mediterranean region
  d. to explain the history, production, benefits, and use of olive oil

Detail

2. When did the cultivation of olive trees begin around the Mediterranean Sea?
  a. 2,000 years ago
  b. 4,000 years ago
  c. 6,000 years ago
  d. No one knows.

Sequence

3. Which step occurs first in olive oil production?
  a. separating the liquid from the solids
  b. crushing the whole olives
  c. separating the oil from the water
  d. drying the olives under the sun

> **Did You Know?**
>
> Greek people use more olive oil per person than any other people in the world.

Detail

4. Which use of olive oil is NOT mentioned in the article?
  a. money
  b. medicine
  c. soap
  d. paint

Inference

5. Why has the author included information about several studies of olive oil?
  a. to explain the growing interest in olive oil around the world
  b. to show how the biology of Mediterranean people is special
  c. to explain that olive oil is more important for women than for men
  d. to give reasons why olive oil is similar to medicine

B. Classification. Write each answer (**a–e**) in the correct place in the chart.

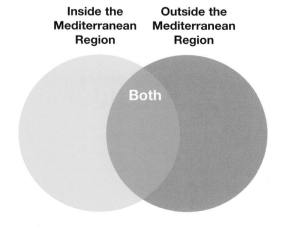

Inside the Mediterranean Region   **Outside the Mediterranean Region**   **Both**

  a. the first production of olive oil
  b. a higher rate of heart disease
  c. olive oil reduces the risk of cancer
  d. the world's top producers of olive oil
  e. enjoy olive oil with meals

☐ Vocabulary Practice

A. Completion. Read the information below. Then complete the sentences with the correct form of the words in red.

Trans fats are specially treated cooking oils often used in the process of preparing various foods sold in restaurants and stores. Until recently, trans fats accounted for nearly all the cooking oil used in fast food restaurants. Recently, as a result of health studies, trans fats have been associated with higher rates of heart disease and with higher chances of getting cancer and other health problems. Based on this new evidence, one American city recently passed a law that limits trans fats to, at most, approximately one half gram in any food product.

1. Water _____ most of our body's weight.
2. Some studies show that eating less food is _____ living longer.
3. The average person eats _____ nine kilograms of beef a year.
4. There is some scientific _____ showing that coffee may help fight certain types of cancer.
5. The _____ of creating trans fats from oil was discovered over 100 years ago.

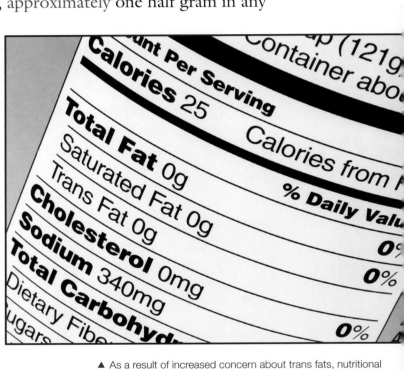

▲ As a result of increased concern about trans fats, nutritional labels on food now show the amount of trans fats it contains.

B. Definitions. Match each word with its definition.

1. attacker _____ **a.** a formal event such as a wedding
2. ceremony _____ **b.** material that is not gas or solid, such as water
3. civilization _____ **c.** first; occurring at the beginning
4. initial _____ **d.** a person who tries to harm another person
5. liquid _____ **e.** a human society with its own culture

Word **Partnership**

Use *evidence* with:
(*v.*) **find** evidence, **gather** evidence, **present** evidence, evidence **to support** (something)

A Taste of the Caribbean

Bernardo's
A Puerto Rican Restaurant

Don't miss these highlights from our kitchen!

1. Deep-fried plantain chips
Start your meal with these light and crisp plantain chips—they're delicious!

2. Shellfish soup
Served in a big pot for sharing, our tasty soup is filled with mussels and other shellfish.

3. Puerto Rican rice and beans
Our rice and beans are flavored with traditional Caribbean ingredients, including sweet chili peppers (called **aji dulce**) and fresh green cilantro (coriander).

4. Baked yams
These sweet yams—called **batatas** in Puerto Rico—are full of natural flavor and are delicious eaten plain.

5. Coconut flan
Try this popular dessert with a Caribbean difference—we've added the sweet taste of coconut!

☐ Before You Read

A. Matching. Read the menu above.
Match each type of food (**1–5**) with its picture.

B. Scan. You are going to read about a type of Puerto Rican food. Quickly scan the reading to answer the questions below. Then read again to check your answers.

1. What kind of dish is *sofrito*? **2.** What do you need to make it?

Sofrito Sensation

1   Puerto Rico, a Caribbean island rich in history and remarkable
natural beauty, has a cuisine[1] all its own. Immigration to the island
has helped to shape its cuisine, with people from all over the world
making various contributions to it. However, before the arrival of
5   these immigrants, the island of Puerto Rico was already known as
Borikén and was inhabited by the Taíno people. Taíno cuisine
included such foods as rodents[2] with sweet chili peppers, fresh
shellfish, yams, and fish fried in corn oil.

Many aspects of Taíno cuisine continue today in Puerto Rican
10   cooking, but it has been heavily influenced by the Spanish, who
invaded Puerto Rico in 1508, and Africans, who were initially
brought to Puerto Rico to work as slaves.[3] Taíno cooking styles were
mixed with ideas brought by the Spanish and Africans to create new
dishes. The Spanish extended food choices by bringing cattle, pigs,
15   goats, and sheep to the island. Africans also added to the island's
food culture by introducing powerful, contrasting tastes in dishes like
piñon–plantains layered in ground beef. In fact, much of the food
Puerto Rico is now famous for—plantains, coffee, sugarcane,
coconuts, and oranges—was actually imported by foreigners
20   to the island.

A common assumption many people make about Puerto Rican food
is that it is very spicy. It's true that chili peppers are popular; *ají
caballero* in particular is a very hot chili pepper that Puerto Ricans
enjoy. However, milder tastes are popular too, such as *sofrito*. The
25   base of many Puerto Rican dishes, sofrito is a sauce made from
chopped onions, garlic, green bell peppers, sweet chili peppers,
oregano, cilantro, and a handful of other spices. It is fried in oil
and then added to other dishes.

How to Make a Basic Sofrito

Ingredients

30

1 yellow onion

2 cloves garlic

1 green bell pepper

3 to 4 sweet chili peppers

3 cilantro (coriander) leaves

35

1 tablespoon olive oil

¼ teaspoon dried whole oregano

Green pepper

Yellow onion

Cilantro

Chili peppers

Oregano

Garlic

Directions

Remove skins from onion and garlic. Clean and prepare green bell and sweet chili peppers. Wash in water.

40 Then finely chop[4] these ingredients, including the cilantro leaves. Place a heavy-bottomed pot over low heat; add oil and oregano. Add the chopped ingredients. Continue cooking for about three to four minutes, stirring[5] occasionally.

▲ Sofrito is used as the base of many Puerto Rican rice, bean, and stewed dishes.

[1] The **cuisine** of a place is its style of cooking.

[2] A **rodent** is a type of small animal such as a mouse or rat.

[3] A **slave** is someone who is the property of another person and has to work for that person.

[4] When you **chop** something, you cut it into small pieces.

[5] When you **stir** something, you mix it.

Reading Comprehension

A. Multiple Choice. Choose the correct answer for each question.

Sequence

1. Who lived in Puerto Rico first?
   a. the Taíno people
   b. the Africans
   c. the Spanish
   d. the Americans

Main Idea

2. What is the main idea of the second paragraph?
   a. Taíno dishes are important in Puerto Rican cooking.
   b. Puerto Rican cooking has had many influences.
   c. Food that has been imported by foreigners isn't really Puerto Rican.
   d. American foods have probably had the most influence.

Reference

3. In line 4, the word *it* refers to
   a. immigration
   b. Puerto Rican cuisine
   c. Caribbean history
   d. the island's natural beauty

> **Did You Know?**
>
> Recent DNA tests showed that more than 60 percent of Puerto Ricans alive today have a connection to the Taíno people.

Detail

4. Which of the following is NOT true?
   a. Many people think Puerto Rican food is spicy.
   b. Puerto Rican cuisine uses a lot of chili peppers.
   c. *Sofrito* is an extremely spicy type of food.
   d. *Ají caballero* is a type of chili pepper.

Detail

5. How is *sofrito* used?
   a. It is eaten before meals.
   b. It is added to other dishes.
   c. It is used when foods are too spicy.
   d. It is eaten as a main dish.

B. True or False. Read the sentences below and circle **T** (true) or **F** (false).

1. The old name for Puerto Rico was Borikén. **T** **F**
2. Pigs were a common ingredient in traditional Taíno cooking. **T** **F**
3. Plantains and sugarcane are native to Puerto Rico. **T** **F**
4. *Sofrito* is traditionally cooked in an oven. **T** **F**
5. Another name for cilantro is coriander. **T** **F**
6. The first ingredients used in preparing *sofrito* are garlic and onions. **T** **F**
7. *Sofrito* should be cooked for at least an hour. **T** **F**

Vocabulary Practice

A. Definitions. Read the information below.
Then match the words in red with their definitions.

Welcome to a world of small, beautiful works of
art that you just can't stop yourself from eating:
the world of Thai sweets. The mildness of this
aspect of Thai cuisine provides some relief from the delicious but spicy main
dishes. The base of Thai sweets—perhaps rice, coconut, banana, or
mango—gives them a lovely taste that says "Thailand." Colorful little sweets
shaped like bananas, apples, mangoes, and oranges are even more beautiful
and delicious than the real thing. Lovely rice cakes called *kanom chan* have
layers of green, white, and pink, or are shaped like flowers. If you travel
through Thailand on a hot day, you may occasionally see a child holding a
colorful treasure in a plastic cup. It's delicious Thai flavored ice–*nam kang sai*.
If you prefer ice cream, coconut is the most popular among Thais, although
traditional imported flavors such as vanilla or strawberry are also well-liked.

▲
Mango with
sticky rice is a
popular and
delicious dessert
in Thailand.

1. _____ one of the parts of something's character or nature
2. _____ happening sometimes, but not very often
3. _____ brought into a country from another country
4. _____ the main or most important part of something
5. _____ material that lies between two other things

B. Completion. Complete the paragraph using the correct form of the words in the
box. One word is extra.

layer	remarkably	immigration	assumption	invade	contrast

When the Spanish **1.** _____ the island of Puerto Rico late in the
15th century, the near destruction of Taíno civilization was the result. With such
2. _____ levels of technology, the Taíno had no chance of winning
the war, and little of surviving at all. In fact, there was a(n) **3.** _____
that the Taíno had completely disappeared, until recent studies showed otherwise.
Although **4.** _____ has brought people from many parts of the
world to Puerto Rico, a large percentage of Caribbean people have been discovered
to have Taíno blood. **5.** _____, several words we use today,
including *tobacco* and *barbecue,* come from the Taíno language.

Usage

When **contrast** is used as a noun, the accent is on the first syllable:
*The **con**trast between the two cultures could not be greater*. As a
verb, the accent is on the second syllable: *The wooden houses in this
part of the city con**trast** sharply with the steel and glass buildings*.

Greek Olives

A. Preview. How much do you know about olives? Are the statements below true (**T**) or false (**F**)?

1. Green, black, and brown olives each
come from a different type of tree.　　　**T**　　**F**

2. The olive branch is a symbol of peace.　**T**　　**F**

3. Olive trees are very easy to recognize.　**T**　　**F**

▲ an olive on a branch

B. Summarize. Watch the video, *Greek Olives*. Then complete the summary below using the correct form of words from the box. Two words are extra.

liquid	approximate	process	associate
evidence	account for	civilization	aspect
initial	remarkable	assume	base

On the Greek island of Naxos, olives grow in many different sizes and colors. Many people
1. _____ make the **2.** _____
that they come from different kinds of trees, but this is incorrect. However, it is usually black olives that are
3. _____ in order to produce oil.

Greeks love olives, and Greece **4.** _____ a lot of the world's olive production. The history of Greek
5. _____, for example, in ancient stories of gods and goddesses, makes clear the importance of the olive to the Greeks. Today, around the world, the olive branch is now
6. _____ with peace and the end of wars.

Another important **7.** _____ of the olive is the
8. _____ benefits which olive oil is said to have for health. There is even **9.** _____ that this amazing
10. _____ can reduce the risk of serious diseases, such as cancer.

C. Think About It.

1. In what ways is olive oil useful? Do you think you will try to eat more olives now?

2. What other foods do you know that have health benefits?

 To learn more about food around the world, visit elt.heinle.com/explorer

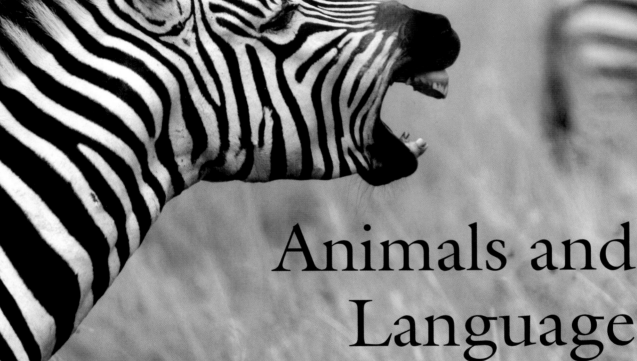

UNIT2

Animals and Language

Discuss these questions with a partner.

1. Which animals do you think are the most intelligent?

2. What are some ways in which animals communicate with each other?

3. Do you think animals have their own languages? If so, do you think humans can learn those languages?

▲ A zebra with its mouth open appears to be talking to another zebra in Masai Mara, Kenya.

1

2

Ocean
Giants

3

2A

☐ Before You Read

A. Matching. The whales in the pictures are humpback whales, some of the most interesting whales in the ocean. Match each description below with the picture it describes.

_____ a. A calf humpback whale holds on to its mother with its **flippers**.

_____ b. Humpback whales cooperate to drive **schools** of small fish to the surface.

_____ c. A humpback whale, flippers extended, begins to sing.

B. Predict. Why do you think humpback whales are popular with whale watchers? Read the first paragraph of the passage to check if you were right.

Song of the Humpback

▲ Jason Sturgis of Whale Trust, a Maui-based research group, photographs a female humpback swimming with her child.

1   Herman Melville, the writer of the famous whale story Moby Dick, wrote that humpback whales were "the most lighthearted[1] of all the whales." A favorite of whale watchers everywhere, they swim in ocean areas close to land and are active at the surface, often jumping out of
5   the water and coming down with a great splash. They are intelligent animals and can be seen working together as they hunt schools of small fish. And, if you listen closely, you might even hear one singing.

Recording Gentle Giants

  Marine biologist[2] Jim Darling has studied the songs of humpback
10   whales for 25 years. While recording whale songs on a boat near Hawaii, he invited author Douglas Chadwick to experience diving with a humpback. In the water, the way Chadwick heard the whale's songs changed completely. "Suddenly, I no longer heard the whale's voice in my ears. I felt it inside my head and bones." He clearly sensed the
15   whale's silent awareness of him. The 13-meter-long giant looked him over[3] curiously, but never harmed him.

  The whale then swam under the boat. It pointed its head down to the ocean floor and, with flippers extended out to its sides, began to sing. Up in the boat, Darling recorded the whale's song. Such songs may
20   be long and complex, lasting for 30 minutes or more; they are perhaps the longest songs sung by any animal.

---

[1] Someone who is **lighthearted** is cheerful and happy.

[2] A **marine biologist** is a scientist who studies ocean life.

[3] If you **look** something **over**, you examine it for a short period of time.

▲ A humpback's song is recorded by an underwater microphone.

Why Do They Sing?

Darling says that only male humpbacks sing, but for unknown reasons. It was previously thought that they sang to attract females, but scientists
25 showed this was incorrect when they played recordings of whale songs in the ocean and no females came around. Another idea is that male humpbacks compete with each other using songs, just as other male animals do using antlers, or tusks.[4]

In addition to their long and mysterious songs, humpbacks make a
30 variety of other sounds as they interact each day. When alarmed by enemies such as killer whales, or when the feeding is especially good, the sounds they produce can be louder than an airplane engine.

A Brighter Future

During the days of heavy whale hunting, the world humpback
35 population was reduced from an estimated 125,000 to around 6,000 animals. Thanks to laws against hunting, humpbacks now number perhaps 30,000 animals, although the constantly moving humpbacks are very difficult to count. However, it now seems that this mysterious singer will
40 continue to sing for years to come.

[4] **Antlers** are long, branched horns that grow on the heads of some animals, like deer or moose; **tusks** are the long, pointed teeth of some animals, like walruses.

Long-distance travelers ▶

In summer months, North Pacific humpbacks feed in the cold waters of Russia, Alaska, and Canada. In winter, three groups travel south to Central America, Hawaii, and the western Pacific. A single journey may take them more than 4,000 kilometers (2,500 miles)—the longest migration of any mammal.

☐ Reading Comprehension

A. Multiple Choice. Choose the correct answer for each question.

Gist
1. What is this reading mainly about?
   a. how humpbacks communicate with people
   b. humpback songs and what they might mean
   c. the career of a man who is interested in humpbacks
   d. how to record humpbacks in the ocean

Detail
2. Why do humpbacks sing?
   a. to attract females
   b. to compete with other males
   c. to communicate with humans
   d. the answer is not known

Detail
3. Which of the following is NOT mentioned as a situation in which humpbacks make sounds?
   a. when they are frightened
   b. when they have found lots of food
   c. when they interact with each other
   d. when humans enter the water with them

Reference
4. In line 25, *this* refers to _____.
   a. the idea that male humpbacks sing
   b. the idea that male humpbacks sing to attract females
   c. the idea that female humpbacks sing to attract males
   d. the idea that males compete using songs

Vocabulary
5. In line 36, *Thanks to* could be replaced by _____.
   a. As a result of
   b. Grateful to
   c. With respect to
   d. Resulting in

Did You Know?

The tail of each humpback has a different shape. Researchers use this shape to identify the whales they study.

B. Matching. Match the numbers on the left with their meaning in the reading.

1. 25   _____**a.** the number of humpbacks before whale hunting began
2. 30   _____**b.** the number of years Jim Darling has studied humpbacks
3. 6,000   _____**c.** the number of minutes a humpback song can last
4. 30,000   _____**d.** the number of humpbacks today
5. 125,000   _____**e.** the number of humpbacks at their lowest point

☐ Vocabulary Practice

Blue whales, like this one off the coast of Mexico, are the largest whales in the ocean.
▼

A. Definitions. Read the information below. Then complete the definitions using the words in red.

Another variety of singing whale is the blue whale. Like humpbacks, blue whales sing songs that marine biologist Phillip Clapham describes as "probably the most complex in the animal kingdom." Although they are the largest whales in the ocean, blue whales can move as fast as 48 kilometers per hour when interacting with other whales. However, this speed couldn't help them escape from their human enemies, who hunted them until they nearly disappeared last century.

Happily, laws now protect blue whales, and their numbers are increasing again. Curious to know more about them, National Geographic scientists have connected cameras to blue whales in the ocean. The cameras, which don't hurt the whales, have given scientists valuable information about the ways blue whales swim, eat, and sing. This information helps scientists better understand and protect blue whales.

1. acting in ways that affect one another _____
2. having many parts and difficult to understand _____
3. those who hate or want to hurt each other _____
4. a type of something _____
5. wanting to learn or know _____

A group of pilot whales beached on the shore of Cape Cod, U.S.A. in 1902. The reason why whales sometimes beach themselves is unknown, but one possibility is that their sonar system sometimes becomes confused. ▼

B. Completion. Complete the information below using the correct form of words from the box. One word is extra.

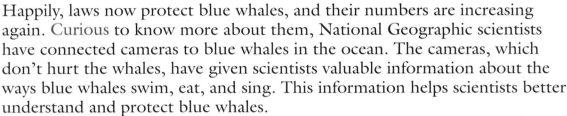

| enemy | harm | awareness | unknown | alarm | constant |

Some whales use sound to get information about the world around them. By **1.** _____ sending out clicking sounds that hit underwater objects and come back, whales receive lots of information. This way of using sound is called *sonar*. Recently, whale lovers have been **2.** _____ by the probability that whales are seriously **3.** _____ by the powerful sonar used by navy ships. The problem is being studied, and people's level of **4.** _____ of the problem is higher than ever before. Although the exact effect of sonar on whales is still **5.** _____, ships around the world are trying to be more careful when using sonar.

Usage

Both **alarm** and **harm** can be used as a noun and a verb. e.g. *to alarm (somebody); to cause alarm; to harm (somebody); to cause harm*

Our Bond with Dogs

▲ Eleven breeds of dogs wait to be photographed.

☐ Before You Read

A. Discussion. Look at the picture and answer the questions.

1. How many types of dogs in the picture can you name?

2. Which are sometimes used as working dogs?

3. Do any of these dogs have special abilities?

4. Which dogs do you think make the best pets? Why?

5. Have you seen any of these types of dogs on TV or in movies?

B. Scan. Scan the passage to find and circle three names that owners gave to their dogs. What type of dog is each one?

▲ Excited sled dogs get ready for the start of the Itarod Dog Race, Alaska, U.S.A.

Dogs
in a human world

1 The partnership between humans and dogs began perhaps 14,000 years ago. Our first interactions may have occurred when wild dogs
5 were attracted to human garbage, or humans may have acquired the puppies[1] of wild dogs and trained them to be obedient pets. By means of the careful selection
10 of dog parents, humans have been able to create a wonderful variety of dogs with plenty of talents and many different looks. Here are three examples of "a dog's life"
15 in the human world.

The working dog

Jacques is one of many beagles that work at airports for the U.S. government in a program known as the Beagle Brigade. Beagles were chosen for this
20 work because of their powerful noses. Their job is to smell and alert officers to illegal fruits, vegetables, and other foods in luggage or in mail. They do the job far better than humans could alone.

▲ A beagle uses its nose to find meat and other illegal items in U.S. mail.

25 Some of the beagles who work in the program are donated by private owners, but many are ownerless beagles rescued from animal shelters.[2] Many beagles who were scheduled to be euthanized[3] are now working to keep their country safe from disease.

Treated like a queen

▲ Tiffy, a Maltese, enjoys a life of luxury on Manhattan's Upper East Side.

30 Tiffy, a beautiful eight-pound[4] maltese is treated like a queen in New York City. Her owner, NancyJane Loewy, carefully prepares her meals of lamb, steak, salmon, tuna, chicken, and a variety of fresh vegetables.
35 Tiffy also gets low-fat yogurt and cookies after dinner. Why? Loewy replies, "I have a dog because the dog needs me."

Leowy, whose husband has a high-paying job and whose two sons are away at school, has the time and money to treat Tiffy extremely
40 well, and she truly enjoys doing so. "I want to give her the healthiest, most wonderful life possible for as long as possible."

The animal carer

▲ Jessie, a specially trained whippet, is a welcome visitor for patients at the National Institutes of Health, Maryland, U.S.A.

Jessie is a whippet that visits children who are fighting deadly diseases. She brightens
45 patients' days with love and gives children a chance to exercise. At the National Institutes of Health, Jessie helps patients like young Lukas Parks to stay strong during their long hospitalization.

50 Whether as workers or objects of affection,[5] dogs have certainly proven themselves to be beneficial to humans in many ways. At the same time, their special place as "man's best friend" has allowed dogs to survive in a human world. While wolves and wild dogs have nearly disappeared from the earth, domestic dogs continue to grow
55 in number, thanks to their special relationship with humans.

---

[1] **Puppies** are young dogs.

[2] An **animal shelter** is a place where animals that are lost or have no owners are kept.

[3] An animal that is **euthanized** is painlessly killed.

[4] **Eight pounds** = 3.6 kg.

[5] **Affection** is fondness or liking for somone.

Reading Comprehension

A. Multiple Choice. Choose the correct answer for each question.

Gist

1. The author's purpose in writing is ___.
 a. to propose that dogs be better cared for
 b. to compare the work of humans and dogs
 c. to show examples of how dogs interact with humans
 d. to illustrate how dogs have not changed over many years

Detail

2. Which of the following is NOT mentioned in the passage?
 a. dog attraction to human garbage
 b. the use of dogs to protect their owners
 c. the training of wild puppies
 d. the selection of dog parents

Vocabulary

3. In line 9, *By means of* could be replaced with ___.
 a. Toward
 b. As a result of
 c. Despite
 d. Without

Did You Know?

The first creature to go into space was a dog. In 1957, the Soviet Union sent a dog named Laika up in a rocket to circle the earth.

Reference

4. In line 39, *doing so* refers to ___.
 a. looking after her sons
 b. taking her dog to school
 c. treating her pet well
 d. having a high-paying job

Detail

5. Which dog eats human food?
 a. Tiffy the Maltese
 b. Jacques the beagle
 c. Jessie the whippet
 d. all of them

B. Classification. Match each phrase with the dog or dogs it describes.

 a. is a working dog
 b. works with children
 c. works for the government
 d. receives lots of love
 e. is treated like a human

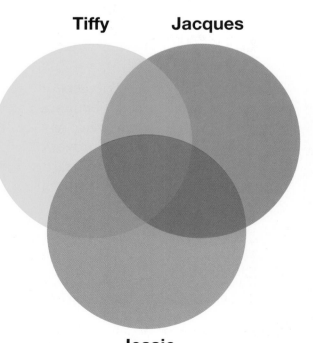

Tiffy   **Jacques**

Jessie

☐ Vocabulary Practice

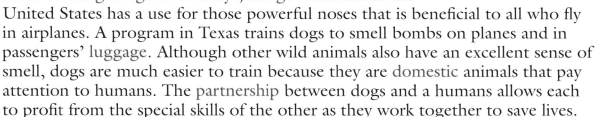

Aron, a German ▶ shepherd, is trained to work for the U.S. government.

A. Matching. Read the information and match each word in red with its definition.

Dogs were probably first attracted to humans by the smell of our garbage. Nowadays, the government of the United States has a use for those powerful noses that is beneficial to all who fly in airplanes. A program in Texas trains dogs to smell bombs on planes and in passengers' luggage. Although other wild animals also have an excellent sense of smell, dogs are much easier to train because they are domestic animals that pay attention to humans. The partnership between dogs and a humans allows each to profit from the special skills of the other as they work together to save lives.

1. bags you carry your belongings in when you travel _____

2. trash _____

3. the people and institutions that rule and control a country _____

4. not wild _____

5. a close relationship often involving working together _____

B. Completion. Complete the information using the correct form of words from the box. One word is extra.

select	acquire	obedient	plenty	talent	domestic

Looking for a guard dog?

Are you thinking about spending a lot of money to **1.** _____ a guard dog to protect your home or business? Did you know that any dog can learn to follow orders? Most can be trained to be completely **2.** _____ in just about two weeks—it doesn't require any special **3.** _____. However, not just any dog can be a guard dog. At the Guard Dog Training Center, our knowledge and experience allow us to find only those dogs with the special qualities necessary to be guard dogs—fearless dogs with a strong desire to protect homes and owners. We have **4.** _____ of excellently trained dogs, including a wide **5.** _____ of doberman pinschers, German shepherds, and rottweilers for you to choose from. They are ready to start protecting your home or business today.

Man's Best Friend

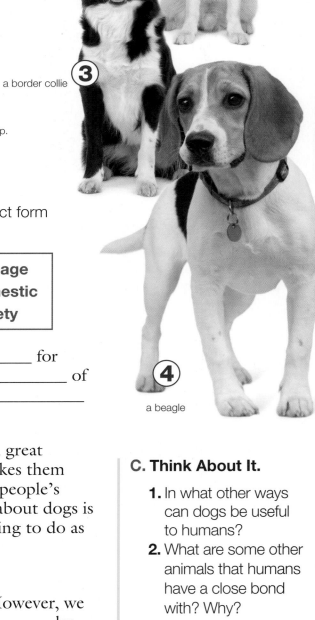

a wolf

a husky

a border collie

a beagle

A. Preview. Match each dog **(1–4)** with a statement.

___ a. pulls people through the cold and snow

___ b. is the animal that all dogs come from

___ c. finds illegal items in luggage

___ d. herds[1] livestock[2]

[1] If you **herd** people or animals somewhere, you make them move there in a group.

[2] **Livestock** are animals such as cattle and sheep which are kept on a farm.

B. Summarize. Watch the video, *Man's Best Friend*. Then complete the summary below using the correct form of words from the box. Two words are extra.

selection	partnership	harm	luggage
plenty	unknown	constant	domestic
interact	obedient	talent	variety

Dogs and humans have had a(n) **1.** _____ for thousands of years. Dogs have a wide **2.** _____ of skills, which they use to help humans in **3.** _____ of different ways.

Dogs have very powerful noses, and they have a great **4.** _____ for smelling things. This makes them good at finding lost people, and illegal items in people's **5.** _____. The most important thing about dogs is that they are very **6.** _____, rarely failing to do as they are told.

How and why humans and dogs first began **7.** _____ is still **8.** _____. However, we do know that thousands of years of **9.** _____ by humans has slowly changed the wolf into the **10.** _____ dog we have today. However the relationship began, it is today clearly beneficial to both humans and dogs.

C. Think About It.

1. In what other ways can dogs be useful to humans?

2. What are some other animals that humans have a close bond with? Why?

To learn more about animals and language, visit elt.heinle.com/explorer

UNIT 3

History
Detectives

WARM UP

Discuss these questions with a partner.

1. Do you think it is important to learn about the past?

2. How do researchers learn about the past? What kinds of evidence do they use?

3. Which past civilizations do you know? What do you know about them?

3A

Secrets of the Pharaohs

▼ Tutankhamun's _____ in the Valley of the Kings.

The golden _____ of Tutankhamun.

Part of the _____ of Tutankhamun.

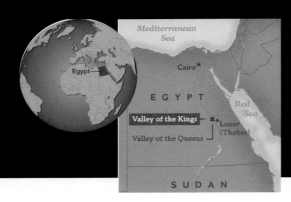

Mediterranean Sea

Egypt

Cairo★

E G Y P T

Red Sea

Valley of the Kings

Luxor (Thebes)

Valley of the Queens

S U D A N

☐ Before You Read

A. Completion. Look at the pictures and read the information below. Complete the captions using the words in **blue**.

On November 4, 1922, British **archeologist** Howard Carter discovered the **tomb** of King Tutankhamun. Inside, a beautiful solid gold **coffin** contained the **mummy** of the body of a young Egyptian king who had died over 3,200 years before.

B. Scan. What are some theories for how Tutankhamun died? Quickly scan the passage, then compare your list with a partner.

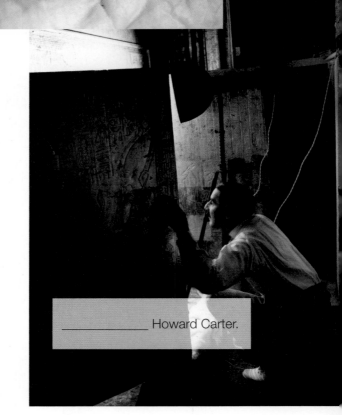

_____ Howard Carter.

Was King Tut Murdered?

1   King Tutankhamun was just a teenager
    when he died. He was the last king of
    a powerful family that had ruled Egypt
    for centuries. When he died in 1322 B.C.,
5   Tut (as Tutankhamun is often known
    today) was placed in a luxurious, gold-
    filled tomb. There he lay forgotten until
    the tomb's eventual discovery in 1922.
    Although we now know a lot about his
10 life, the reason for Tutankhamun's death
    at such a young age has remained a
    mystery, with murder the most extreme
    possibility. Now, improved X-ray
    technology[1] is offering new clues into
15 King Tut's death.

▲ Is this the face of Tutankhamun? Recent
analysis allows us to recreate, for the first
time, what the boy king looked like.

Discovered and Damaged

The British archeologist Howard Carter opened
Tut's tomb in 1922. Although it had been robbed
in ancient times, it was still full of gold and other
20 amazing items. Carter spent months carefully
recording the treasures. When he and his team
then attempted to remove King Tut's
mummy, they found that it had become
attached to its solid gold coffin.
25 Unfortunately, they did a great deal
of damage to the mummy
while removing it.

▲ **Secrets Revealed**
To reach Tut's body, Carter's team had
to open up four boxes, or shrines, and
three mummy-shaped coffins—one of
solid gold—all tightly packed within a
stone tomb.

[1] **X-ray technology** is a special
way of taking pictures of the
inside of something.

◄ "When I saw his face, I was shocked," says Zahi Hawass. "My heart was pounding, and I could not speak."

Theories About Tut's Death

In 1968, archeologists conducted an examination of the mummy using
30   simple x-ray technology. Three important discoveries led to various theories about his death.

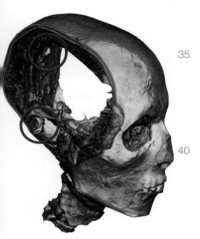

▲ Two loose pieces of bone (circled) may have broken off when Tut's body was being made ready for burial, or during its removal by Carter's team. It's unlikely the damage was caused by a blow to the head.

- The X-rays showed that bones in King Tut's chest[2] were missing. Carter hadn't done that damage. Tut was a trained fighter and
35   hunter, so some people have guessed that it was caused by a war injury or a hunting accident.
- There appeared to be pieces of bone inside the skull, causing many to believe that King Tut was killed by a blow from behind to the head. Was he murdered by people wanting to take control of Egypt?
40
- A serious fracture discovered above Tut's left knee could have been the result of an accident or attack. Infection might have started there and killed the boy king.

A Closer Look at the Mummy

In recent years, scientists, under the direction of Zahi Hawass, head of
45   Egypt's Supreme Council of Antiquities,[3] have applied a new and more effective X-ray technology to mummies throughout Egypt. In the images, each bone appears in perfect detail.

So, was King Tut's death murder or accident, infection or war injury? Doctors who analyzed the X-ray images say that the skull was mainly
50   undamaged, excluding the possibility of a blow to the head. However, while modern technology has been able to rule out one theory, the actual cause of death remains unknown. It seems there are secrets that even the latest technology cannot yet find the answers to.

[2] Your **chest** is the top part of the front of your body.

[3] Egypt's **Supreme Council of Antiquities** is responsible for the care and protection of Egypt's historic treasures.

Reading Comprehension

A. Multiple Choice. Choose the correct answer for each question.

Gist
1. How does the article answer the question, "Was King Tut murdered?"
  a. He was probably murdered.
  b. He probably died in an accident.
  c. How he died is still not known.
  d. He died from a blow to the head.

Detail
2. Which of the following has NOT been suggested as a reason for King Tut's death?
  a. He died in an accident.
  b. He was killed in a robbery.
  c. He died from an infection.
  d. He was murdered.

Detail
3. How was the mummy of King Tut damaged?
  a. It was damaged by x-ray technology.
  b. It was damaged when it was placed in the tomb.
  c. It was damaged when it was removed from the coffin.
  d. It was damaged during a war in Egypt.

Detail
4. What was the problem with King Tut's chest?
  a. Bones were missing from it.
  b. It was damaged in war.
  c. An accident had damaged it.
  d. Carter had removed bones from it.

> **Did You Know?**
>
> The mummy of King Tutankhamun still rests in a glass case in the tomb where Howard Carter first found him.

Vocabulary
5. In line 51, the phrase *rule out* is closest in meaning to _____.
  a. suggest
  b. confirm
  c. question
  d. exclude

B. Matching. Label the timeline below with the events.

1. Images of King Tut's mummy are taken with simple x-ray technology.
2. King Tut's tomb is robbed.
3. Howard Carter discovers King Tut's tomb.
4. More effective X-ray technology is applied to mummies in Egypt.
5. King Tut is placed in a gold-filled tomb.

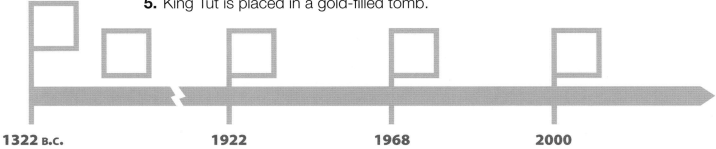

1322 B.C.   1922   1968   2000

Vocabulary Practice

A. Completion. Complete the information using the correct form of words from the box. One word is extra

exclude	attach	theory	luxury	conduct	injury

A man dressed as the god Anubis prepares a body for mummification in this ancient Egyptian wall painting.

The pharaohs of ancient Egypt lived very **1.** _____ lives, and it seems that they wanted to take their treasure into the next life, too, because their tombs were filled with beautiful items of gold. In the ancient Egyptians' complex **2.** _____ of life after death, their body had to last a very long time. This is the reason for mummies. In the mummification process the liquid was removed from the body, which was then treated with oil and spices, and covered in cloth to **3.** _____ any water—mummies must be kept dry to last. Thanks to tests **4.** _____ by researchers, we have been able to learn a lot about the pharaohs—how they looked, whether they had any **5.** _____, and more!

▼ Mummy found in South Korea

B. Completion. Complete the information using the correct form of words from the box. One word is extra.

analysis	attach	infect	luxury	murder	teenager

A group of mummies recently unearthed in South Korea may offer hope for treating a deadly modern-day illness. They also tell of an ancient love story. One of the well-preserved bodies shows evidence of being **1.** _____ by the hepatitis B virus. Scientists hope that **2.** _____ of the body will help them understand more about this deadly disease.

Another body was found together with several poems written by his wife. The man has been identified as the son of a senior official who may have been involved in a plan to **3.** _____ the emperor.

The 500-year-old love poems have similarities to *Romeo and Juliet*, Shakespeare's famous play about two **4.** _____ in love. The man's wife writes of her strong **5.** _____ to her husband, even beyond his death:

I cannot live without you anymore.
I hope I could be with you.
Please let me go with you.
My love to you, it is unforgettable in this world,
and my sorrow,[1] it is without end.

[1] **Sorrow** is a feeling of extreme sadness.

Word Link

teen = from 13 to 19: eigh**teen**, seven**teen**, **teen**ager, **teen** magazine

The Iceman's quiver and arrows.

The Iceman was carrying this stone knife when he died.

A fire-starting kit and other tools found on Iceman.

POLICE REPORT

"Iceman" mummy found in Italian Alps

CONDITION OF MUMMY:
Nearly perfect condition, but deep cuts on hand and one on back

APPROXIMATE AGE AT DEATH:
Mid-forties

APPROXIMATE TIME OF DEATH:
5,300 years ago

CLOTHES:
Three layers of clothes and bearskin shoes

PERSONAL POSSESSIONS:
Stone dagger, valuable copper axe, half-finished wooden arrows, fire-starting kit

OTHER:
A dark object visible in body under left shoulder

A Body in the Mountains

☐ Before You Read

A. Discussion. A mummy was found high in the Alps in Italy. Use the information in the police report above to help you answer the questions below. Discuss your answers with a partner.

1. How long ago did the "Iceman" actually die?
   a. recently   b. hundreds of years ago   c. thousands of years ago

2. Did he die naturally or was he murdered?
   a. naturally   b. murdered

3. What do you think the dark shape under his shoulder is?
   a. blood   b. a tattoo   c. part of an arrow

B. Scan. Now scan the reading passage to see if your predictions are correct.

Who Killed the Iceman?

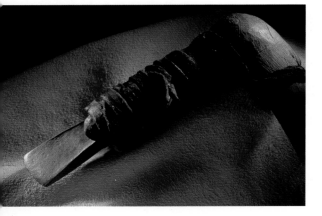

New evidence ▶ suggests that a 5,300-year-old man found frozen in the Alps may have been murdered.

▲ The Iceman carried this ax with him on his final journey.

1 In 1991, high in the mountains of Europe, hikers made a gruesome[1] discovery: a dead man partly frozen in the ice. However, the police investigation soon became a scientific
5 one. Carbon dating[2] indicated that the man died over 5,300 years ago. Today he is known as the Iceman and has been nicknamed "Ötzi" for the Ötztal Alps where he was found. Kept in perfect condition by the ice,
10 he is the oldest complete human body on earth.

Who Was the Iceman?

Scientists think he was an important person in his society. An examination of his teeth and
15 skull tells us that he was not a young man. His arms were not the arms of a laborer. His dagger was made of stone, but he carried a copper[3] ax. This implies wealth, and he was probably from the upper classes.[4] We know he
20 could make fire, as a fire-starting kit was discovered with him. Even the food he had eaten enabled scientists to deduce exactly where in Italy he lived.

[1] Something that is **gruesome** is unpleasant and shocking.

[2] **Carbon dating** is a scientific method of finding out exactly how old an object is.

[3] **Copper** is a soft, reddish-brown metal.

[4] The **upper classes** are the group of people in a society who own the most property and have the highest social level.

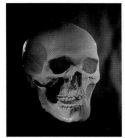

Clues to an Ancient Murder

25 But why did the Iceman die in such a high and icy place?
There have been many theories. Some said he was a lost
shepherd.[5] Others thought he was killed in a religious
ceremony. Over the years since he was found, tiny scientific
discoveries have led to great changes in our understanding
30 of the story of the Iceman. The newest scientific information
indicates that he was cruelly murdered. "Even five years ago,
the story was that he fled[6] up there and walked around in the
snow and probably died of exposure,[7]" said Klaus Oeggl, a
scientist at the University of Innsbruck in Austria. "Now it's
35 all changed. It's more like a… crime scene."

A Bloody Discovery

In June 2001, an X-ray examination of the body showed a
small dark shape beneath the Iceman's left shoulder. It was
the stone head of an arrow. It had caused a deadly injury that
40 probably killed him very quickly. In 2003, an Australian
scientist discovered the blood of four different people on the
clothes of the Iceman. Did a bloody fight take place before his
murder? Injuries on his hand and head indicate that this may
be true. One theory, put forward by archeologist Walter
45 Leitner, says that the Iceman's murder was the end of a
fight for power among his people. However, this idea is
certainly debatable.

Today, the research continues, proving some theories false while
opening the door to others. Through scientific research, this
50 oldest member of our human family continues to tell us about
his life and the time in which he lived.

[5] A **shepherd** is a person, usually a man, whose job is to take care of sheep.
[6] To **flee** means to escape.
[7] **Exposure** is the harmful effect on your body from very cold weather.

▲ Using detailed scans,
scientists are able
to recreate what the
Iceman may have
looked like.

◀ The Iceman's
body was found
at a pass in the Ötztal Alps,
between Austria and Italy. He had
started his journey 20 kilometers
(12 miles) to the south, in the Val Venosta.
Why he was traveling so high in the
mountains is still a mystery.

☐ Reading Comprehension

A. Multiple Choice. Choose the correct answer for each question.

Gist   **1.** What is this reading mainly about?
    a. how people murdered others long ago
    b. what scientists have learned about a death long ago
    c. the reasons why mummies can last so long in the mountains
    d. the reasons why theories about the Iceman are often wrong

Detail   **2.** Why do scientists believe the Iceman was not a young man?
    a. His clothes were those of an older man.
    b. He was an important person in his society.
    c. He had powerful arms.
    d. His teeth and skull were of an older man.

Detail   **3.** What probably caused the death of the Iceman?
    a. an axe
    b. a dagger
    c. an arrow
    d. a knife

> **Did You Know?**
>
> The Iceman has approximately 57 tattoos on his body. They are just simple dots and lines.

Reference   **4.** The word *this* in line 43 refers to the fact that _____.
    a. the Iceman had a head injury.
    b. the Iceman was in a fight.
    c. there was blood on the Iceman's clothes.
    d. the Iceman died very quickly.

Vocabulary   **5.** In line 49, what does *opening the door to* mean?
    a. allowing the possiblity for
    b. excluding the chance of
    c. disproving
    d. providing evidence for

B. Fact or Theory? Which of these statements about the Iceman are facts (**F**) and which are theories (**T**)?

_____ **a.** He was found in the mountains.
_____ **b.** He had a fight before his murder.
_____ **c.** His murder was the end of a fight for power.
_____ **d.** He died over 5,300 years ago.
_____ **e.** He had an injury on his hand.

An artist's painting of the last ▶ moments of the Iceman as he dies alone in the snow

Vocabulary Practice

A. Completion. Complete the information with the correct form of the words in the box. One word is extra.

wealth	laborer	freeze	cruel	debatable	tiny

1. After shooting the Iceman, his murderer may have _____ pulled out part of the arrow and left him to die.

2. The Iceman lived before the invention of money; in his time _____ meant fine tools, clothing, houses, and animals.

3. Scientists believe that Ötzi was not a(n) _____ because his body is in good condition and doesn't show the damage caused by a life of hard work.

4. Many scientists now believe that the cause of Ötzi's death was the _____ arrowhead, only two centimeters across, found under his shoulder.

5. Although there are many interesting ideas about how the Iceman died, the truth about his death remains _____.

B. Definitions. Read the information below. Then complete the definitions using the correct form of the words in red.

Scientists really wanted to understand how the Iceman's body could last over 5,000 years. At first they thought that he had dried out, like mummies in Egypt. However, the Iceman had no hair, and a layer of his skin was gone. Scientists knew that Egyptian mummies still have their hair and skin. The knowledge of this difference enabled scientists to deduce that a different process must have happened to the Iceman. Scientists also knew that bodies that stay beneath the water for a long time lose their hair, which implies that the Iceman's body had been under the water before it was dried out and frozen in the ice.

1. Something that is under another thing is _____ it.

2. If you _____ something, you reach that conclusion because of other things that you know to be true.

3. If something is _____, it has become very hard because of the cold.

4. If an event or situation _____ that something is true, it makes you think that it is true.

5. If something _____ you to do a particular thing, it makes it possible for you to do it.

Word Partnership

Use *debate* with:
open to debate, **major** debate, **political** debate,
presidential debate, debate **over something**,
debate **the issue**

Inca Mummy

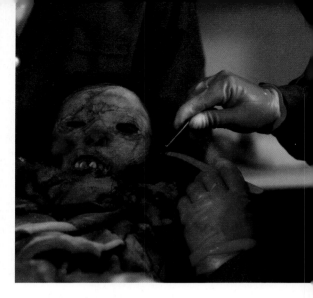

A. Preview. Look at this picture of the mummy of a girl found dead on a peak[1] in the Andes mountains. How do you think she died? Choose **a**, **b**, or **c**.

a. She was killed by attackers from another country.

b. She was sacrificed[2] to the mountain god.

c. She died after getting lost in the mountains.

[1] A **peak** is a mountain or the top of a mountain.

[2] To **sacrifice** an animal or person means to kill them in a special religious ceremony as an offering to a god.

▲ Peruvian mummy expert Sonia Guillen examines the Inca mummy's hair.

B. Summarize. Watch the video, *Inca Maiden*. Then complete the summary below using the correct form of words from the box. Two words are extra.

analyze	beneath	enable	freeze
conduct	theory	attach	deduce
exclude	injury	luxurious	murder

In 1995, Johan Reinhard and his team found a mummy while they were **1.** _____ an archeological investigation on a mountain peak in the Andes. From the evidence they could find, the team was able to **2.** _____ that it was an Inca girl, who they named "Juanita" after Johan. Juanita was **3.** _____ in a religious ceremony. Followers of the religion believed the **4.** _____ that sacrificing humans would please the god of the mountain. Months after the discovery, Juanita was **5.** _____ using modern technology. The researchers discovered a serious **6.** _____ on the side of her head. This was the cause of her death.

Returning to the same mountain, Reinhard's team found even more mummies buried **7.** _____ the ground with clothes and other ancient items. For scientists, the discovery provided plenty of valuable information about the past. It would **8.** _____ them to learn a lot about Inca civilization. Removing the mummies was extremely difficult because everything was **9.** _____ due to the extreme cold, and the mummies had become **10.** _____ to the ground.

C. Think About It.

1. What do you think scientists can learn about the Inca civilization from the mummies?
2. What else do you know about the Inca civilization or other ancient civilizations?

 To learn more about history detectives and archeological discoveries, visit elt.heinle.com/explorer

A. Crossword. Use the definitions below to complete the missing words.

[crossword grid]

Across
1. having many different parts; difficult to understand
3. to cause something to have a disease or illness
5. a number of different kinds of something
7. to say something indirectly
8. a human society with its own culture
11. very unusual or amazing
13. very small
14. related to home and family
15. to hurt or damage
16. money and riches
17. to study carefully
18. to bring into a country

Down
1. to show the differences
2. to prevent from being part of something
4. a natural ability to do something well
6. facts that lead you to believe something is true
8. an event such as marriage or graduation
9. to communicate or work together
10. under
12. to suppose

B. Notes Completion. Scan the information on pages 46–47 to complete the notes.

Field Notes

Site: Ancient cities of _____ and Herculaneum

Location: Campania, _____

Information:
- Formed _____ years ago, Mount _____ has caused several natural disasters, including a huge eruption nearly 4,000 years ago
- The most famous eruption occurred on _____, 79 A.D., when it buried entire cities beneath layers of _____
- Before the disaster, people in Herculaneum enjoyed the heated _____ of the suburban baths
- They also watched actors perform in the _____ and athletes compete in the _____ area
- The buried cities were rediscovered in the _____ century and are still being uncovered today

Buried Cities

Site: **Ancient Cities of Pompeii and Herculaneum**

Location: **Campania, Italy**

Category: **Cultural**

Status: **World Heritage Site since 1997**

"I LOOKED ROUND: A DENSE BLACK CLOUD WAS COMING UP BEHIND US, SPREADING OVER THE EARTH LIKE A FLOOD."

Pliny the Younger
(c.61 A.D. – c.112 A.D.)

Pompeii and Herculaneum

Today it may appear calm and peaceful, but Mount Vesuvius has been responsible for some of the worst natural **disasters** in history. Although evidence shows that Vesuvius has **erupted** many times since its formation approximately 25,000 years ago, most people associate Vesuvius with the huge explosion that occurred on August 24, 79 A.D. The eruption lasted for two days and killed thousands in the ancient Roman towns of Pompeii and Herculaneum. Beneath layers of the volcano's **ash**, the towns—and their people—were frozen in a moment in time.

Rediscovered in the mid-18th century, the remarkably well-preserved remains have enabled archeologists to gain a deeper understanding of Roman civilization. "We're digging in an area where a lot of Pompeians died during the eruption," says archeologist Gary Devore. "I remind myself all the time that I can investigate in such detail this ancient Roman culture as a direct result of a great human disaster."

The eruption that buried Pompeii and Herculaneum was not Vesuvius' worst. Scientists have found evidence of a bigger, more violent eruption in 1780 B.C., which likely killed or injured thousands of people living near the base of the volcano. The timing of the next big eruption remains unknown—although most scientists assume it is not far away.

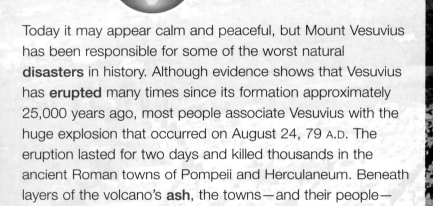

Based on recent findings, this illustration shows what Herculaneum looked like shortly before its destruction by Vesuvius. ▼

1 In the town's **theater**, actors performed in front of crowds of up to 2,500 people.

2 Herculaneum's citizens used the **basilica** to do business or to seek advice on legal issues.

3 At the **palaestra** (sports area), young athletes competed in wrestling, swimming, and races.

4 Only the wealthiest citizens could afford to live in the luxurious **seafront houses**.

5 Religious ceremonies and celebrations took place in the **sacred area**.

6 People came to the **suburban baths** to relax in the heated indoor pools.

◄ The process of uncovering and analyzing the cities' ancient remains began more than 200 years ago, and is still being conducted today.

Glossary

ash: the gray-white material that remains after something has burnt

disaster: a very bad event, such as an earthquake or a plane crash

erupt: to break out suddenly, with force

▲ **Frozen in time:** In 79 A.D. the ancient Roman town of Pompeii was completely buried by an eruption of Vesuvius, the world's most dangerous volcano.

A Global View

Across the globe, over 6.7 billion people speak more than 5,000 languages. Each language is distinct, shaped by the cultures and people who use it. However, **linguists**—people who study and analyze language—have found evidence that some languages that sound and look very different actually have many similar aspects.

These groups of similar languages are called **language families**. Linguists have deduced that the languages in each family evolved from a single original language. Over time, when speakers of these ancient tongues interacted with other cultures or migrated to other parts of the world, they spread their language across the globe. Today aspects of the original language can be found in the various languages spoken by their descendants.

Indo-European

The largest language family, with approximately 500 languages and three billion speakers, includes English, German, Spanish, and Hindi, a language spoken by about one-fifth of India's population. Originating in what is now southern Russia, this giant language family has been carried by exploration and colonization all over the world.

Major language families today

- Afro-Asiatic
- Altaic
- Austro-Asiatic
- Austronesian
- Dravidian
- Indo-European
- Japanese/Korean
- Kam-Tai
- Niger-Congo
- Nilo-Saharan
- Sino-Tibetan
- Uralic
- Other

Top Ten Languages

Some languages have only a few hundred speakers, but others have millions. China's **official language**, Mandarin, has approximately 874 million **native speakers** (people who learned it as a first language rather than as a foreign language). Spanish, English, and Portuguese are also widely spoken—largely as a result of large overseas empires built by the European nations. English is now widely used in fields such as science and international business. The total number of English speakers in the world (including non-native speakers) is debatable; estimates range from 500 million to more than a billion.

Native speakers (in millions)

Language	Value
Chinese (Mandarin)	873
Spanish	322
English	309
Arabic	220
Hindi	180
Portuguese	177
Bengali	171
Russian	145
Japanese	122
German	95

Languages

Afro-Asiatic

The languages of ancient Babylon and Egypt belonged to this family, which includes 375 languages spoken throughout Africa and South-west Asia. Its largest **living language** is Arabic, the language of Islam, spoken by over 200 million people worldwide.

Japanese/ Korean

These two languages were heavily influenced by Sino-Tibetan, which has eight distinct Chinese languages. Both Japanese and Korean imported Chinese words, and modern Japanese still uses written Chinese symbols, or **characters**.

Moscow

London
Paris *EUROPE* *ASIA*

Beijing

Tokyo

Cairo

AFRICA Mumbai
(Bombay)

Lagos

Jakarta

AUSTRALIA

Sydney

Native American

In the Americas, most people speak dominant Indo-European languages like English, Spanish, and Portuguese. However, some native languages have survived. Quechua, the **mother tongue** of the Inca, still has ten million speakers, and in Paraguay, Guarani is still in daily use.

Word Partnership

Use *language* with: **body** language, **computer** language, **programming** language, **sign** language, **foreign** language.

Critical Thinking

Evaluating
As the world's population increases, the number of languages decreases. What might be the negative aspects to this? Could there be any advantages?

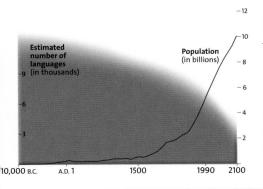

Estimated
number of
languages
(in thousands)

—9

-6

-3

Population
(in billions)

—12

—10

—8

—6

—4

—2

10,000 B.C.   A.D. 1   1500   1990 2100

Language Death

There are many dying or **dead languages**— languages that people no longer speak or understand. Linguists estimate that 10,000 languages once existed, but fewer than 5,000 are understood or spoken today. And while Earth's population is growing, the number of living languages is declining at an alarming rate.

A Global View   **49**

A. Definitions. Use words in **bold** from pages 48–49 to complete the sentences.

1. Written symbols called _____ are used in languages such as Chinese and Japanese.

2. _____ are people who study the way language works.

3. A _____ is a group of languages that have a common origin.

4. The _____ of a country is one that is approved by its government.

5. Your _____ is the language that you grew up speaking.

6. A _____ of English is someone who learned it as a first language rather than as a foreign language.

7. A _____ is a language that is used by people today.

8. A language that is no longer used by anyone is known as a _____.

B. Word Link. The suffix **–en** changes certain adjectives to verbs, adding the meaning "make" or "become." The suffix **–ness** changes adjectives to abstract nouns. Complete the chart with the verb and noun forms of the adjective. Then use the correct form of the words to complete the passage.

After several days in the desert, the archeologist's eyes had _____ due to the _____ of the air and the _____ of the sun. As he approached the tomb entrance, his heartbeat began to _____. After entering the tomb, the archeologist soon found the king's coffin. He expected the lid to be difficult to lift, but was surprised at its _____. However, he was _____ by what he found inside: the king's body was no longer there.

Adjective	Verb	Noun
1. bright	*brighten*	*brightness*
2. sad		
3. light		
4. red		
5. quick		
6. dry		

UNIT 4

Great Destinations

Discuss these questions with a partner.

1. What overseas travel destinations are popular with people from your country?

2. What destinations should a visitor to your country make sure to see?

3. How many different forms of transportation have you used?

Which do you like most? Why?

4A

Big City Travel

At the heart of Manhattan Island is New York's famous Central Park. Here are some of the highlights visitors should not miss:

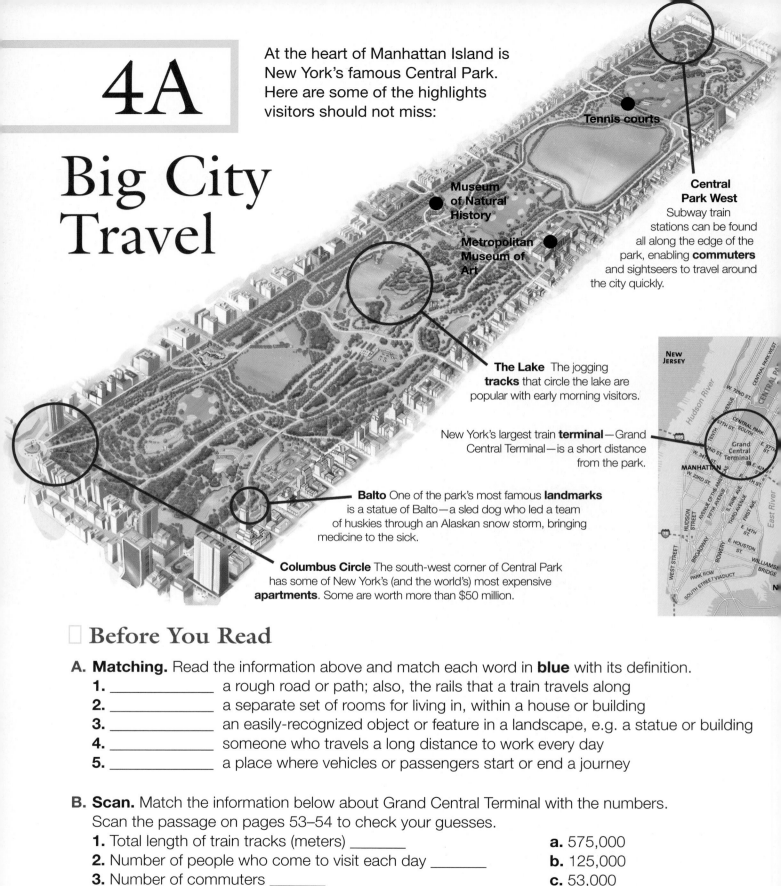

Tennis courts

Central Park West Subway train stations can be found all along the edge of the park, enabling **commuters** and sightseers to travel around the city quickly.

Museum of Natural History

Metropolitan Museum of Art

The Lake The jogging **tracks** that circle the lake are popular with early morning visitors.

New York's largest train **terminal**—Grand Central Terminal—is a short distance from the park.

Balto One of the park's most famous **landmarks** is a statue of Balto—a sled dog who led a team of huskies through an Alaskan snow storm, bringing medicine to the sick.

Columbus Circle The south-west corner of Central Park has some of New York's (and the world's) most expensive **apartments**. Some are worth more than $50 million.

☐ Before You Read

A. Matching. Read the information above and match each word in **blue** with its definition.

1. _____ a rough road or path; also, the rails that a train travels along
2. _____ a separate set of rooms for living in, within a house or building
3. _____ an easily-recognized object or feature in a landscape, e.g. a statue or building
4. _____ someone who travels a long distance to work every day
5. _____ a place where vehicles or passengers start or end a journey

B. Scan. Match the information below about Grand Central Terminal with the numbers. Scan the passage on pages 53–54 to check your guesses.

1. Total length of train tracks (meters) _____
2. Number of people who come to visit each day _____
3. Number of commuters _____
4. Meals served in terminal restaurants each day _____

a. 575,000
b. 125,000
c. 53,000
d. 10,000

Grand Central Terminal

1 Everything about Grand Central Terminal (GCT), conveniently located in the heart of Manhattan, is remarkable. On an average day, 700,000 people pass in and out of it. The information booth in the Main Concourse (the huge room that is the focal point of the building) gets as many as

5 a thousand visitors an hour. Standing beside it, you feel that if you stood there long enough you would eventually see every person you have ever known in your life. "It's the town square for eight million people," says GCT spokesperson Dan Brucker. "If people get separated in the city, they'll meet at the information booth."

10 GCT's art and style reflect the great economic success of railroad companies before the growth of car and air travel. You could spend years in Grand Central before you discovered all its secrets: its tennis courts, its hidden railroad cars, its private ground-floor apartment (now a bar). Nine stories below the lowest floor that the public gets to

15 see is a basement known as M-42. Brucker explains, "This is not just the deepest and the biggest but the most secret basement in the city. During World War II, there were shoot-to-kill orders if you showed up down here."

20 It was where the power came from to move the trains carrying soldiers. Today, one box in the basement holds a small red button, about the size of a coin. Above it is written

25 "Emergency Stop." If you pressed this button, says Brucker, you could "make 125,000 people late for dinner."

▲ Rushing travelers fill the Main Concourse of Grand Central Terminal, New York City.

◄ "It's the town square for eight million people," says GCT spokesman Dan Brucker.

This hidden underground platform, ▶ located near Grand Central, is said to have been used as a secret passage by President Franklin D. Roosevelt in the 1940s.

Above the ground, the Main Concourse features a ceiling painted to
30 look like the night sky, with stars shining down. Over the years, smoke blackened this beautiful ceiling. Although people thought smoke from trains was the cause, it was actually tobacco smoke! However, it has since been cleaned and now shows its original beauty.

In the name of modernization, plans were made to destroy GCT in the
35 1960s. However, many people objected, and finally New Yorkers decided GCT was worth saving. In 1976, the U.S. government agreed. It made GCT a National Historic Landmark,[1] recognizing its importance for all Americans and ensuring its continued protection. Once threatened with destruction, Grand Central Terminal continues to give pleasure to
40 passengers and sightseers in Manhattan.

Grand Central Terminal by the numbers

Size: Covers 20 hectares of land (almost 30 soccer fields), 53 kilometers of track, and 44 platforms—more than any other station in the world
Commuters: About 125,000 a day
45 **Visitors:** Some 575,000 people a day come just to eat, shop, and sightsee
Oldest business: The Oyster Bar, opened in 1913, the same year as GCT
Meals served in terminal restaurants: 10,000 a day
Newspaper recycled: Over 4,500 kilograms a day
Percentage of trains on time: 98
50 **Items in Lost and Found:** 19,000 a year

▲ GCT's Lost and Found Office gets more than 200 lost cell phones a month.

[1] A **National Historic Landmark** is a building, place, or structure that the U.S. government has officially decided to be of historic importance.

▲ About 125,000 travelers arrive at Grand Central every day.

Reading Comprehension

A. Multiple Choice. Choose the correct answer for each question.

Detail

1. Which statement is NOT true about Grand Central Terminal?
a. It is one of the world's largest train stations.
b. It has more commuters than visitors each day.
c. It was built before the growth of car and air travel.
d. It is in the heart of Manhattan.

Did You Know?

Grand Central Terminal has been featured in scenes in many movies, including *North by Northwest, The Fisher King,* and *Madagascar.*

Detail

2. What was blackened by smoke?
a. the hidden railroad cars
b. the ceiling of the main concourse
c. the information booth
d. basement M-42

Inference

3. Which of the following statements would Dan Brucker most likely agree with?
a. Grand Central Terminal needs more information booths.
b. People who go to Basement M-42 today might be shot.
c. Grand Central Terminal is a focal point of New York City.
d. The "Emergency Stop" button should be removed.

Vocabulary

4. The phrase *showed up* in line 19 is closest in meaning to _____.
a. appeared   c. spoke
b. displayed something   d. demonstrated

Purpose

5. What is the main purpose of this article?
a. To discuss the importance of rail travel.
b. To introduce an important New York landmark.
c. To interview Dan Brucker.
d. To argue for the importance of National Historic Landmarks.

B. Completion. Complete this letter written by a sightseer to Grand Central Terminal. Use no more than two words from the passage to fill in each blank.

Dear Mom,

I'm writing you from Grand Central Station. As many other people do, I've come to meet a friend by the **1.** _____. I never need to buy a

2. _____ in Grand Central Station—the recycling boxes are full of them. The ceiling above is really beautiful now, but it used to be dirty from **3.** _____. I'm meeting a friend for lunch at The Oyster Bar, which is actually the **4.** _____ in the terminal.

She's late, but I don't mind waiting and writing to you in this beautiful National **5.** _____.

Love, Julie

Vocabulary Practice

A. Completion. Complete the information using the correct form of the words in the box. One word is extra.

sightseer	threaten	economic	convenient	locate	modernize

▲ There are now more than 2,000 National Historic Landmarks in the United States. Over 10 percent, including the Statue of Liberty, are in New York State.

The National Historic Landmarks program chooses structures, places, and things **1.** _____ mostly in the United States that are important to America's history. Although this is a government program, the government doesn't own the landmarks, and 16% of them are in danger, **2.** _____ with loss or destruction.

Owners of the landmarks do not always have enough money to keep them in good condition or to fight against people who don't care about such history and feel that **3.** _____ them or replacing them with new structures is best. Protecting such landmarks can be expensive, and while some money can be collected from **4.** _____ who visit, the National Historic Landmarks Program tries to reduce some of this **5.** _____ pressure by giving money to landmark owners.

B. Words in Context. Complete each sentence with the best answer.

1. A feature of a building is _____.
   a. a problem with it   b. an important part of it

2. If transportation is convenient, it is _____.
   a. easy to use   b. clean and modern

3. A focal point is a location that is _____.
   a. central and important   b. built very well

4. To touch the ceiling of a room, you need to _____.
   a. bend down   b. reach up

5. If you object to something, you say that you _____.
   a. agree with it   b. do not like it

▲ Not all the National Historic Landmarks are within the United States. Some, like Nan Madol, a stone monument on Ponape Island, Micronesia, are in other countries.

Word Partnership

Use *location* with:
central location, **convenient** location, **secret** location, **exact** location, **geographic** location, **present** location

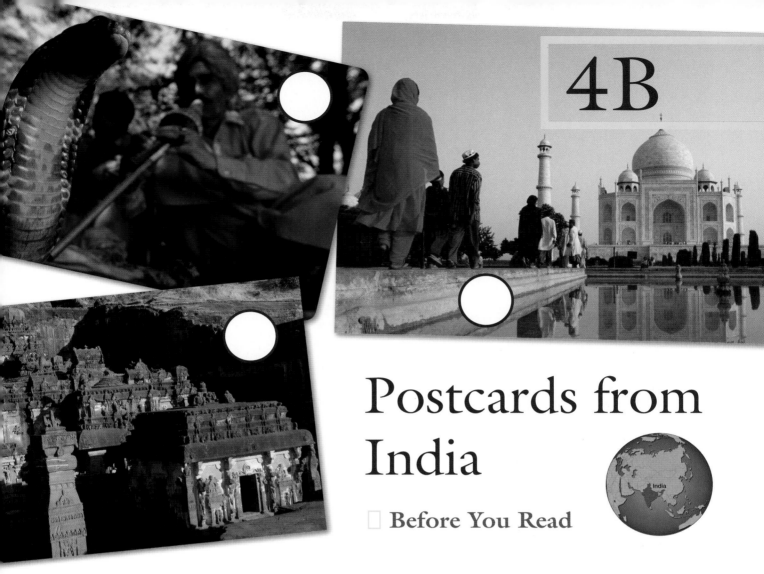

Postcards from India

☐ **Before You Read**

A. Matching. Read the sentences and match each word in **blue** with a definition. Then number the postcards (**1–3**).

1. Snake charmers and a **diverse** range of other performers can be found on the streets of New Delhi, India's capital city.

2. The rock-cut Kailash temple, located among India's Ellora Caves, contains many **impressive** stone **sculptures**.

3. Visitors walk toward one of the world's most famous **monuments**—the Taj Mahal, near Agra, India.

a. _____ varied; made up of many different parts
b. _____ having a strong effect on the mind or emotions
c. _____ large structures built to remind people of famous events or people
d. _____ works of art created by shaping stone, wood, or other materials

B. Scan. What was the city of Mumbai named for? Scan the reading and check (✔) your answer.

☐ a movie   ☐ a goddess   ☐ an island   ☐ a queen

Mumbai: City of Dreams

◀ **Mumbai's Chowpatty Beach** provides a relaxing contrast to the city's vibrant crowds and traffic.

1 The vibrant[1] city of Mumbai is a natural first stop for visitors to India's western coast. "One could say that Mumbai is the New York of India," says Mumbai native Divya Abhat. "It's a place of big opportunities, big contrasts, and big energies . . . There is always something going on."

5 Previously known as Bombay, the city was renamed Mumbai (derived from the goddess Mumba) in 1995 as part of a movement away from colonial[2] names. The traditional cultural center of India, Mumbai is today a very modern city with world-class shopping, restaurants, and business areas. It is also home to Bollywood, the world's largest movie industry.

10 India is a complex country, culturally rich and diverse. If you visit India, be prepared for sensory overload;[3] you will experience a culture of amazing 15 depth and variety.

▼ A woman and her son walk past a Bollywood poster on a Mumbai street corner.

[1] If something is **vibrant**, it is full of life and energy.

[2] **Colonial** refers to countries that are controlled by another country.

[3] **Sensory overload** occurs when there is too much information for our senses to manage.

Here are just a few of
Mumbai's sights
that visitors should not miss:

20   Five-star luxury can be enjoyed at **Mumbai's Taj Mahal Palace Hotel**, built
in 1903 by Persian[4]-Indian businessman Jamsetji Tata. According to local
legend, Tata was not permitted to enter the finest British-managed hotel of
that time, Wilson's, because of its policy of serving only European guests.
In response, he established the Taj, with a promise that it would have the
world's best service. Ever since, the Taj
25   Mahal Palace has been listed among the
world's top hotels. What about Wilson's?
It's long gone.

Across the street from the Taj is the famous
Gateway of India, an arch standing about
30   25 meters high. The monument was built to
celebrate the visit to India of England's
King George V and Queen Mary in 1911.
Sellers and performers, including snake charmers,
can be found in the surrounding busy park. At night,
35   lit up by electric lights, the Gateway appeals to
sightseers—and lovers, too!

▲ The Taj Mahal Palace Hotel (left) and
the Gateway of India (right) are two of
Mumbai's most famous monuments
and serve as reminders of the city's
colonial heritage.

Just a one-hour ferry ride from Mumbai is
the island of **Elephanta**. The island was
named by the Portuguese, supposedly after
40   a huge statue of an elephant that used to be
there. It has amazing cave temples cut deeply
into the rock, featuring sculptures preserved
since the seventh century A.D.

Visitors leaving Mumbai can board their train
45   at the **Victoria Terminus** (renamed Chhatrapati Shivaji
Terminus). This remarkable station is said to have been
India's largest construction project when it was built in
1888. An impressive mixture of British and Indian building
styles, the station is preserved today as a World Heritage Site.

▲ The 19th-century Victoria Terminus
(Chhatrapati Shivaji Terminus)
is preserved today as a World
Heritage Site.

---

[4] **Persian** means related to the area now known as Iran.

☐ Reading Comprehension

A. Multiple Choice. Choose the correct answer for each question.

Gist
1. One could say that Mumbai is the New York of India because _____.
   a. it is home to India's film industry.
   b. it is a highly populated center for business and culture.
   c. it has moved away from its colonial past.
   d. it was once controlled by the British.

Detail
2. According to a local legend, why did Jamsetji Tata establish his hotel?
   a. A British-managed hotel wouldn't let him stay.
   b. He loved Wilson's Hotel and wanted to build something like it.
   c. It had been his dream since he was a child.
   d. He wanted to create a Persian-Indian style hotel.

Detail
3. Which of the following is NOT mentioned about the Gateway of India?
   a. It is about 25 meters high.
   b. It is lit by electric lights at night.
   c. It was built by the English.
   d. It has a busy park around it.

> **Did You Know?**
>
> The last British troops left India through the Gateway of India arch in 1948.

Inference
4. What language is "Elephanta" probably from?
   a. English   c. an Indian language
   b. Portuguese   d. Persian

Purpose
5. What kind of reader is this passage most likely intended for?
   a. foreign tourists   c. Mumbai residents
   b. historians   d. business people

B. Classification. Are the following related to Colonial India, to Independent India, or to both? Write each answer (**a–g**) in the correct place in the chart.

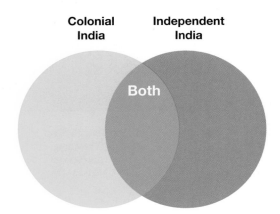

Colonial India   Independent India   Both

   a. the building of the Gateway of India
   b. the city name Mumbai
   c. Bollywood
   d. the city name Bombay
   e. The Taj Mahal Hotel
   f. Wilson's
   g. Victoria Terminus becomes a World Heritage Site

Vocabulary Practice

A. Matching. Read the information below.
Then match each word in red with its definition.

Bollywood, Mumbai's famous film industry, was established in 1913, when the first movie was made there. Its name is derived from *Bombay*, the colonial name of Mumbai, and *Hollywood*, the American movie making center. Of the 1,000 or more Bollywood movies made today, most are musicals that include a mixture of song, dance, love, comedy, and action. Song and dance scenes by the male and female stars are often performed in impressive structures or surrounded by nature. Bollywood movies appeal to people all over the world. Bollywood movies are especially popular in the many areas of the world that have been populated by Indians and that have a cultural connection with India, such as South Africa, Nigeria, and Morocco.

▲ Popular Indian star Deepika Padukone is photographed at the London opening of Bollywood film *Om Shanti Om*.

a. related to the arts, ideas, and customs of a particular society _____

b. developed or obtained from something else _____

c. be attractive or interesting for (someone) _____

d. having (something) all around _____

e. begun or created _____

B. Completion. Complete the sentences with the correct form of words from the box. One word is extra.

permitted	policy	cultural	supposedly	preserve	cave

1. The word *Bollywood* was _____ invented by a journalist, although it isn't sure exactly who that journalist was.

2. Tourists are advised to ask before taking pictures at holy places around Mumbai, as photography may not be _____.

3. Hidden under the ground in the _____ at Ajanta, India are paintings and sculptures representing some of the finest examples of religious art.

4. Mumbai's Sanjay Gandhi National Park is dedicated to the _____ of the forest and animals such as leopards, deer, and monkeys.

5. Among the _____ investigated to help solve Mumbai's air pollution problems are switching to cleaner-running city buses, and increasing gasoline taxes.

Word Partnership

Use *policy* with: **economic** policy; **foreign** policy; **government** policy; **immigration** policy; **a change of** policy

Mountain Train

A. Preview. Read the information and guess the answers to the questions.

The train in the picture burns coal and turns water into steam[1] for power. It is very old, and moves slowly down winding[2] mountain tracks.

1. The train is known as _____.
   a. the Toy Train   b. the luxury train

2. How do most people feel about riding such a slow train?
   a. They like it.   b. They want a faster one.

[1] When water boils it creates **steam**.

[2] A **winding** road is not straight and has lots of turns.

▲ The Darjeeling Himalayan Railway

B. Summarize. Watch the video, *Mountain Train.* Then complete the summary below using the correct form of words from the box. Two words are extra.

appeal	**locate**	**focus**	**modernization**
convenient	**preserve**	**establish**	**derive**
sightseer	**permit**	**cave**	**surround**

Darjiling
India

In contrast to the **1.** _____ of trains occurring around the world, the Darjeeling Himalayan Railway still runs very slowly. The railway was **2.** _____ in 1881, and has been carefully **3.** _____ by the local people. Some people call it the "Toy Train." Today the train **4.** _____ to both local people and **5.** _____ who come from other places to see the railway and the **6.** _____ mountains. It may not be the most **7.** _____ train, but many of the passengers seem to **8.** _____ a lot of pleasure from its slow speed, which **9.** _____ more time to see the amazing views. In fact, there is a sign **10.** _____ near the train line which says "Slow has got four letters, so has life . . . speed has got five letters, so has death."

C. Think About It.

1. Why do you think the local people have preserved the Toy Train?

2. Which of the places in this unit would you most like to visit? Why?

To learn more about travel adventures and great destinations, visit elt.heinle.com/explorer

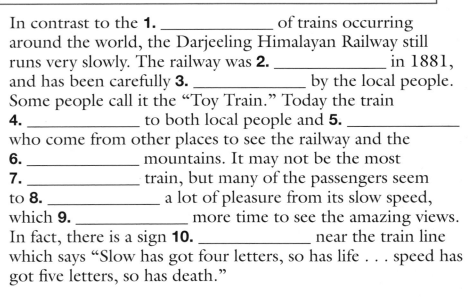

UNIT 5

Storms

WARM UP

Discuss these questions with a partner.

1. Have you ever experienced a very serious storm?

2. What kinds of damage can storms do?

3. What parts of the world have the worst storms?

▲ A huge wave from a storm crashes on
a sea wall in front of a luxury home in
Groton, Connecticut, U.S.A.

63

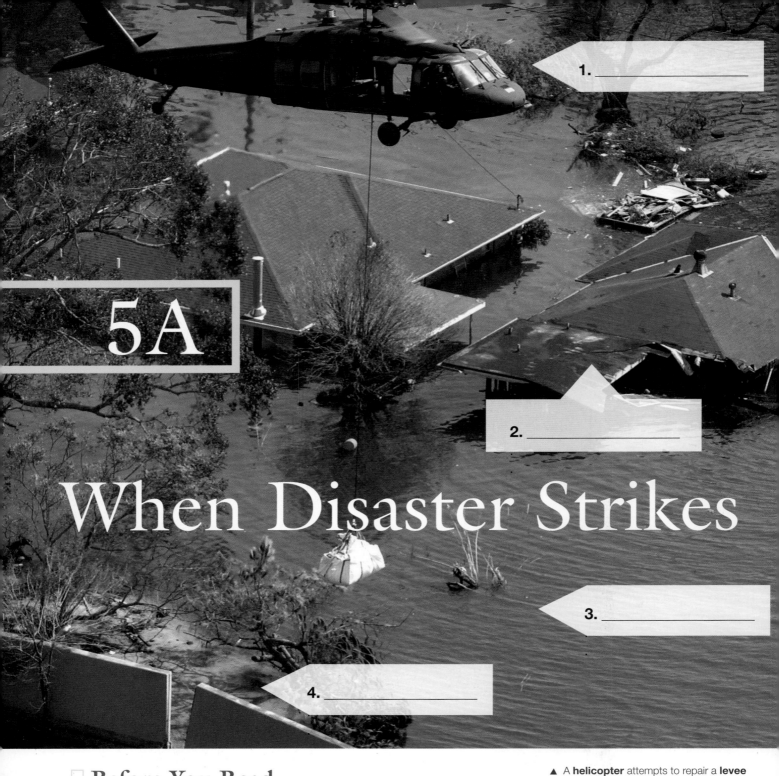

5A

When Disaster Strikes

1. _____

2. _____

3. _____

4. _____

▲ A **helicopter** attempts to repair a **levee** holding back the water during the **flooding** of New Orleans. Many people were forced up to their **roofs** where they waited for help.

☐ Before You Read

A. Matching. Look at the picture and read the caption. Label the items in the photo using the words in **blue**.

B. Discussion. Discuss these questions.

1. The photo above was taken in New Orleans, U.S.A., in 2005. What do you think caused the flooding?
2. How do you think people were affected by the flooding?

The Flooding of New Orleans

1 Hurricane Katrina, which struck the U.S. Gulf Coast in August 2005, was one of the costliest natural disasters[1] in U.S. history—both economically and in terms of lives lost. Damage to the city of New Orleans was estimated at more than 22 billion dollars.

5 Over one million people were forced out of the city, and nearly 1,500 people lost their lives.

▲ The city of New Orleans lies under water following one of the costliest disasters in U.S. history.

The Storm Arrives

A day before Hurricane Katrina passed close to New Orleans, residents were ordered to leave the city. Unfortunately, tens of thousands of people ignored the

10 order or were unable to leave. When Hurricane Katrina hit, water broke through the system of levees and flood walls constructed by government engineers. Many people in low-lying sectors of the city were forced up onto their roofs by the flood water and waited for help to come by boat or helicopter.

Chaos[2] in the City

15 Circumstances soon grew worse. There were not enough police left in the city, so people were not only exposed to dangerous floodwaters but also to widespread crime. "Most of our people were focused on getting people off roofs and out of the water," said one police officer. "There were not enough people in the city to rescue and distribute food and water to those who needed help."

20 Looting[3] of stores was common. "I've looted," said Matthew, 35. "But only to keep my family and myself alive. They left us here for days without any food or water, like we were just supposed to die. So we had to loot or die."

---

[1] A **disaster** is a very bad accident.

[2] **Chaos** is a state of complete disorder and confusion.

[3] **Looting** is stealing from stores or houses during times of great confusion, such as during a war or natural disaster.

Waiting for Help

A borrowed hotel curtain hung over
street signs provided shelter for one large
extended family. "I was starting to think
it was going to be our home forever,"
Kenneth, 47, said. "They told us every
day that buses were going to take us to
shelters.[4] It was just lies and more lies."

People lived without running water or
toilets as they waited for help. Dead
bodies were left on streets. It was days
before the government gained control
of the city and the remaining people
were taken to safety.

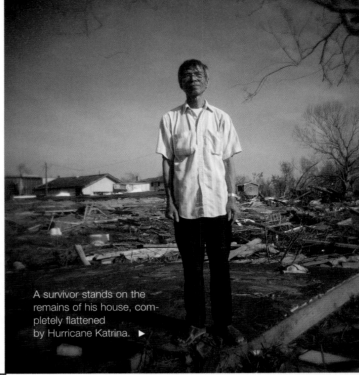

A survivor stands on the remains of his house, completely flattened by Hurricane Katrina. ▶

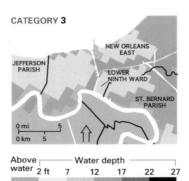

Houses were thrown against the Mississippi levees by the hurricane's power. ▶

Should New Orleans Be Rebuilt?

Some experts believe that rebuilding
New Orleans isn't a good idea.
Currently, even a hurricane of average
strength could cause flooding in the
city again. Global warming is raising
sea levels each year, and to make things
worse, the land beneath New Orleans
is sinking at a rate of up to 2.5
centimeters a year. However, despite
the risk, two-thirds of the people who
left have returned to help rebuild the
city they love.

Storm Warnings ▶
A computer model predicts the damage
that will occur if another hurricane hits New
Orleans. A Category 5 hurricane could easily push storm waters over the levees and
flood the entire city; even a Category 3 storm
would affect large areas of the city.

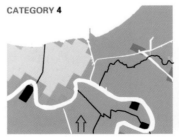

CATEGORY **3**

NEW ORLEANS EAST

JEFFERSON PARISH

LOWER NINTH WARD

ST. BERNARD PARISH

0 mi — 5
0 km — 5

CATEGORY **4**

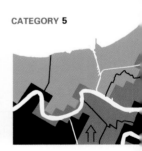

CATEGORY **5**

Above water — Water depth —
2 ft   7   12   17   22   27

⇑ 15 mph storm heading north

[4] A **shelter** is a place where people without
homes can stay for a limited period of time.

Reading Comprehension

A. Multiple Choice. Choose the correct answer for each question.

Gist

1. What is this passage mainly about?
   a. how Katrina formed
   b. why New Orleans should be rebuilt
   c. how people in New Orleans died in Katrina
   d. the impact of Katrina on New Orleans

Detail

2. How many people lost their lives in the flooding of New Orleans?
   a. 22
   b. 300
   c. 1,500
   d. 2005

Detail

3. Which of the following is NOT a factor that made the disaster worse?
   a. water breaking through the levees
   b. looting and other crime
   c. slow distribution of food and water
   d. people returning to the city

Vocabulary

4. In line 46, the phrase *up to* is closest in meaning to _____.
   a. more than
   b. as high as
   c. from
   d. approximately

> **Did You Know?**
>
> Thousands of pets were lost during the flooding of New Orleans. Many of their pictures were put on websites so that their owners could find them.

Main Idea

5. What is the main idea of the last paragraph?
   a. Many people cannot understand why rebuilding New Orleans is a good idea.
   b. Many people think that global warming isn't actually happening.
   c. Many people don't believe what experts say about rebuilding New Orleans.
   d. Many people love their city so much they will risk more flooding.

B. Sequencing. In what order did the following events occur? Number them from **1** to **5**.

_____ **a.** People were forced up to their roofs.
_____ **b.** A number of stores were looted.
_____ **c.** Water broke through the system of levees and flood walls.
_____ **d.** The government gained control of the city and took people to safety.
_____ **e.** Everyone was ordered to leave the city.

Vocabulary Practice

A. Completion. Complete the information using the
correct form of words from the box. One word is extra.

▲ Walls like this are
very important in
protecting low-lying
areas of the Netherlands
from flooding.

currently	distribute	reside	ignore	sector
widespread	circumstances	sink	engineer	exposed

The Dutch are used to living in a country which is always **1.** _____ to the
dangers of deadly floods. A country with half of its land below sea level cannot afford
to **2.** _____ the problem of rising sea level, and Holland, which already has
about U.S. $2.5 trillion invested in flood prevention, plans to invest as much as U.S.
$25 billion more over the next century. Life in these challenging **3.** _____
has inspired the Dutch to develop many excellent methods of fighting floods. In fact,
during the flooding of New Orleans, the tiny country of Holland sent flood-fighting
equipment and machinery which was **4.** _____ to the brave people
fighting the high waters there. Thanks to the skill of Dutch **5.** _____,
flooding in Holland is rarely **6.** _____, and is instead contained to certain
7. _____ of the country. Two such areas are the valleys of the Rhine and the
Meuse Rivers. Despite large flood walls, these rivers regularly flood the surrounding
areas. During dry times, however, those areas are perfectly pleasant to **8.** _____
in. One solution that is being developed is a type of house that seems normal in
every way, except that it can float during times of high water rather than simply
9. _____ beneath the waves as normal houses would. Groups of houses
would form floating neighborhoods in which people could live together during
times of high water, temporarily getting around by boat until the end of the flood.

B. Definitions. Use the correct form of the words in the box in **A** to complete the definitions.

1. If something is _____, it is moving slowly downward.
2. If someone _____ somewhere, they live there or are staying there.
3. _____ are the conditions which affect what happens in a particular situation.
4. _____ work in designing and constructing engines and machinery or structures.
5. If someone is _____ to something dangerous or unpleasant, they are put
in a situation in which it might affect them.
6. If you _____ something, you pay no attention to it.
7. If you _____ things, you hand them or deliver them to a number of people.
8. Something that is _____ exists or happens over a large area.
9. A(n) _____ of a country or a country's economy is a part of it.

Word Partnership

Use **neighborhood** with:
poor neighborhood, **residential** neighborhood,
run-down neighborhood

Superstorm

eye

The strong winds of hurricanes—called typhoons in the western Pacific Ocean and cyclones in the Indian Ocean—get their energy from warm ocean waters, so they disappear quickly over cooler, dryer areas.

NORTH AMERICA

EUROPE

ASIA

PACIFIC OCEAN

June 1–Nov 30, peak: Aug–Oct

Storms all year, peak: Jul–Nov

May–early Nov, peak: Aug–Sep

AFRICA

Apr–Dec, double peak: Apr–Jun; Sep–Dec

Late Oct–May, peak: Feb–Mar

PACIFIC OCEAN

SOUTH AMERICA

ATLANTIC OCEAN

INDIAN OCEAN

AUSTRALIA

Typical tropical cyclone tracks

Late Oct–May, peak: Jan–Feb

Cyclone season, peak months

ANTARCTICA

equator

northern hemisphere

southern hemisphere

Before You Read

A. True or False. How much do you know about tropical cyclones? Are the following statements true (**T**) or false (**F**)?

1. A **hurricane** is a type of tropical cyclone.   T   F

2. Tropical cyclones happen in the **northern hemisphere** but not in the **southern hemisphere**   T   F

3. Tropical cyclones are formed near the **equator.**   T   F

4. The center of a tropical cyclone is called the **eye**.   T   F

B. Scan. Scan the passage to find the words and phrases in **blue** above. Check your answers to the questions in **A**.

Tropical Cyclones

▲ Hurricane Allen attacks the coast of Texas with 160 kph (100 mph) winds.

1 We call them by sweet-sounding names like Firinga or Katrina, but they are huge rotating storms 200 to 2,000 kilometers wide with winds that blow at speeds of more than 100 kilometers per hour. Weather professionals, or **meteorologists**, know them as tropical cyclones, but they are called hurricanes in the Caribbean Sea, typhoons in the Pacific Ocean, and cyclones in the Indian Ocean. They occur in both the northern and southern hemispheres. Large ones have destroyed cities and killed hundreds of thousands of people.

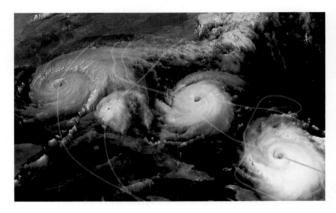

▲ Satellite images of the 2004 hurricane season. Satellite data can help meteorologists predict where hurricanes are heading, but accurate long-term predictions are difficult to make.

Birth of a Giant

15 We know that tropical cyclones begin over water that is warmer than 27 degrees Celsius (80 degrees Fahrenheit) slightly north or south of the earth's equator. Warm, humid air full of water vapor[1] moves upward. The earth's rotation causes the growing storm to start to rotate around its center (called the **eye**). At a certain height, the water vapor condenses,[2] changing to liquid and releasing heat. The heat draws more air and water vapor upward, creating a cycle as air and water vapor rise and liquid water falls. If the cycle speeds up until winds reach 118 kilometers per hour, the storm qualifies as a tropical cyclone.

[1] Water in the form of gas is called **water vapor**.
[2] When a gas or vapor **condenses**, it changes into a liquid.

Storm Surge

Most deaths in tropical cyclones are caused by **storm surge**. This is a rise in sea level, sometimes seven meters or more, caused by the storm pushing against the ocean's surface. Storm surge was to blame for the flooding of New Orleans in 2005. The storm surge of Cyclone Nargis in 2008 in Myanmar pushed seawater nearly four meters deep some 40 kilometers inland, resulting in many deaths.

▼ The powerful winds of a hurricane were strong enough to lift this house onto a car.

Difficult to Predict

The goal is to know when and where the next tropical cyclone will form. "And we can't really do that yet," says David Nolan, a weather researcher from the University of Miami. The direction and strength of tropical cyclones are also difficult to predict, even with computer assistance. Three-day forecasts are still off by an average of 280 kilometers. Forecasters do know that storms are often energized where ocean water is deep and warm, that high waves tend to reduce their force, and that when tropical cyclones move over land, they begin to die.

Long-term forecasts are poor; small differences in the combination of weather factors lead to very different storms. More accurate forecasting could help people decide to evacuate³ when a storm is on the way. "People often return after an evacuation to find nothing really happened," says storm researcher Sharan Majumdar. "The solution is to improve forecasting through better science. That's the only way to get people to trust the warnings."

³ If people **evacuate** a place, they move out of it because it has become dangerous.

Reading Comprehension

A. Multiple Choice. Choose the correct answer for each question.

Detail

1. Firinga is _____.
a. an ocean
c. a storm
b. a large city
d. a famous meteorologist

Did You Know?

Weather forecasting as we know it became possible with the invention of the telegraph in 1837. That allowed news of approaching storms to be communicated faster than the weather itself could arrive.

Vocabulary

2. In line 19, the word *condenses* is closest in meaning to _____.
a. heats up
c. starts rotating
b. moves higher
d. becomes liquid

Sequence

3. Which step comes first in the process of storm formation?
a. Winds reach 118 kilometers per hour.
b. Warm, humid air moves upward.
c. Liquid water falls.
d. Water vapor condenses.

Paraphrase

4. Which of the following is closest in meaning to "the direction and strength of tropical storms are difficult to predict, even with computer assistance" on line 32?
a. Despite using computers, it is difficult to know where tropical cyclones will strike next.
b. Without computers, predicting tropical cyclones is impossible.
c. Computer assistance removes the difficulty of predicting tropical cyclones.
d. Using computers to predict tropical storms is difficult.

Main Idea

5. What is the main idea of the third paragraph?
a. Rising sea levels are causing increasing storm damage.
b. In a storm, most people are killed by high sea levels.
c. People have tried to connect storm deaths to rising sea levels.
d. Dangerous storm surges happen mostly in Bangladesh.

B. Matching. Match the causes on the left with their effects on the right.

Causes	Effects
___ **1.** condensing water vapor releases	**a.** a storm as a tropical cyclone
___ **2.** winds of 118 kilometers per hour qualify	**b.** a storm surge
___ **3.** deep, warm ocean water energizes	**c.** a storm's force
___ **4.** high waves reduce	**d.** heat
___ **5.** storms pushing against ocean surface create	**e.** a storm

Vocabulary Practice

A. Completion. Complete the information with the correct form of words from the box. One word is extra.

combination	upward	cycle	professional	rotate
qualify	energize	forecast	humid	blame

▲ An F3 tornado sets down in a field.

A tornado is a column of quickly rotating air that reaches from the clouds all the way to the ground below. Like their big sisters, the tropical cyclones, tornadoes are formed in upward-moving, warm and **1.** _____ air. Also like tropical cyclones, tornadoes produce strong winds that **2.** _____ around a center of low pressure. Although tornadoes are much smaller than tropical cyclones—the largest being about four kilometers across—their winds can be as fast as 480 kph.

You can't always see a tornado, but it becomes a frightening dark color when it pulls dirt **3.** _____ from the ground. The power of tornadoes is expressed on a scale from F0 to F5. An F0, with wind speeds up to 110 kph, might damage signs, while a tornado with wind speeds of about 420 to 480 kph can blow houses over, **4.** _____ as an F5.

Many tornadoes develop from dangerous, long-lived thunderstorms called *supercells* that are between 10 and 16 kilometers across. Supercells can create tornadoes one after another in a repeating **5.** _____, in which a new tornado forms where the previous one dies.

In the United States tornadoes are to **6.** _____ for a number of deaths every year, sometimes totaling in the hundreds. The National Weather Service attempts to **7.** _____ tornadoes and warns people when they start to form. They advise people to stay in a basement, closet, or bathroom. However, **8.** _____ storm researchers sometimes approach within just meters of tornados to collect information using a(n) **9.** _____ of methods that include computers, video cameras, and their own observations. The 1996 movie *Twister* was about such brave researchers.

B. Definitions. Use the correct form of words in the box in **A** to complete the definitions.

1. If something _____ as something, it has all the features necessary to be that thing.

2. If you _____ a person or thing for something bad, you believe that they are responsible for it.

3. A(n) _____ is a series of events that is repeated again and again in the same order.

4. _____ means relating to a person's work, especially work that requires special training.

5. When something _____, it turns with a circular movement.

6. A(n) _____ of things is a mixture of them.

Word Partnership

Use *qualify* with:
qualify **as** *something*, qualify **for** *something*, **fail to** qualify

Birth of a Hurricane

A. Preview. Combine the suffixes in the box and the words in red to complete the definitions below.

-al	-uction	-ation	-ic

1. A catastrophe is an unexpected event that causes great suffering and damage.
(*n.*) catastrophe; (*adj.*) _____

2. To destroy something means to cause so much damage that it is completely ruined or does not exist anymore.
(*v.*) destroy; (*n.*) _____

3. The tropics are the hottest parts of the world, near the equator.
(*n.*) tropics; (*adj.*) _____

4. When a gas or vapor condenses, it changes into a liquid.
(*v.*) condense; (*n.*) _____

New Orleans, Louisiana

B. Summarize. Watch the video, *Birth of a Hurricane*. Then complete the summary below using the correct form of words from the box. Two words are extra.

upward	widespread	expose	currently
qualify	circumstances	cycle	energize
humid	professional	rotate	combination

The formation of hurricane Katrina depended on a **1.** _____ of a number of different **2.** _____. Warm and **3.** _____ air was moving **4.** _____ into the sky from the warm ocean near the Bahamas. As more air rose and lower ocean air took its place, a **5.** _____ of continuously moving air was started. Condensation resulted in the creation of rain and more warming of the already warm air.

Thunderstorms were created high above and began to **6.** _____ around the center of the new storm. As the storm moved slowly into the waters of the warmer water of the Gulf of Mexico, it was **7.** _____ even more. When its winds reached 73 kilometers per hour, Katrina could be called a tropical storm.

By the time Katrina hit the United States, it **8.** _____ as a Category 4 hurricane. The two places that were the most **9.** _____ to the powerful winds were the states of Louisiana and Mississippi. In those two states, destruction was **10.** _____.

C. Think About It.

1. What lessons can we learn from Hurricane Katrina?
2. What natural disasters occur in your country? How do people and the government respond to them?

To learn more about storms, visit elt.heinle.com/explorer

UNIT 6

Reef Encounters

Discuss these questions with a partner.

1. What do you like most about the ocean?

2. Do you think humans have damaged parts of the world's oceans? How?

3. Which ocean animals do you think are dangerous?

▲ An arrow blenny (*Lucayablennius zingaro*) pokes its head out of an opening of a sea plant, waiting for prey. Caribbean Sea, Cuba.

75

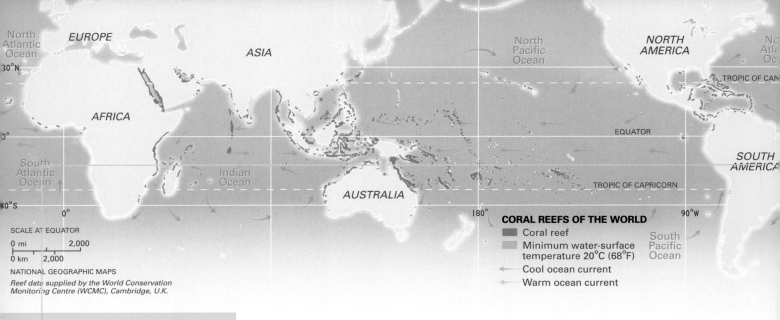

CORAL REEFS OF THE WORLD

■ Coral reef
■ Minimum water-surface temperature 20°C (68°F)
← Cool ocean current
← Warm ocean current

SCALE AT EQUATOR

0 mi   2,000
0 km   2,000

NATIONAL GEOGRAPHIC MAPS
Reef data supplied by the World Conservation
Monitoring Centre (WCMC), Cambridge, U.K.

6A Coral Reefs

☐ Before You Read

A. True or False. Look at the map and read the sentences (**1–4**). Circle **T** (True) or **F** (False). Correct the statement if it is false.

   1. Most of the world's coral reefs are located near cool ocean currents.   **T**   **F**
   2. There are many reefs in the seas of Southeast Asia and Australia.   **T**   **F**
   3. Coral is mostly found where sea temperature is less than 20°C.   **T**   **F**
   4. Most coral reefs are found between the Equator and the Tropics.   **T**   **F**

B. Predict. Look quickly at the title, headings, photos, and captions on pages 77–78. Check (✔) the information you think you'll read about.

   ❑ How coral is formed
   ❑ Coral reef wildlife
   ❑ Problems affecting reefs
   ❑ Threats to coral fishermen

Cities Beneath the Sea

1　Coral polyps[1] can truly be called the animals that helped make the world. For uncounted generations, trillions[2] upon trillions of coral polyps have built structures called reefs, larger in scale than those of any other living beings, including humans. The stone-like material
5　created by these tiny animals becomes limestone, a prized building material that was used to construct the Great Pyramids of Egypt. Huge deposits of limestone exist underground, beneath the ocean, in islands, and in mountains. Limestone has been used in the construction of countless churches, castles, train stations, and banks, and crushed
10　limestone is a major ingredient of cement.[3]

▲ Egypt's Red Sea coral reefs are home to an amazing variety of species. ▼

A Variety of Life

Living coral reefs are remarkable "cities beneath the sea," filled with a rich variety of life. These undersea ecosystems[4] thrive in the warm, shallow
15　oceans near the equator. Among the world's most colorful places, coral reefs are full of brilliantly colored fish and coral covered in wonderful patterns. Reef fish are an important food source for humans, and make up a significant percentage
20　of the global fish catch.

[1] A **polyp** is a small animal that lives in the sea.

[2] A **trillion** is 1,000,000,000,000.

[3] **Cement** is a gray powder which is mixed with sand and water to make concrete.

[4] An **ecosystem** is a particular area in which plants and animals living together have formed complex relationships.

A diver uses cyanide to collect fish from coral reefs. Traders can receive a high price for reef fish in aquarium markets.

Threats to Coral Reefs

In recent years, various factors have threatened coral reefs and the life that depends on them as their home. Blast fishing is an illegal fishing method which involves setting off bombs in the water to kill as many fish as possible. Its negative effects on a reef are significant; it kills most living things and causes great damage to the reef's structure.

Fishing with liquid cyanide, a very dangerous and deadly material, is another threat to reef ecosystems, particularly in the Philippines. Fishermen release liquid cyanide into the reef and collect the stunned[5] fish, which are then sold for big money to the aquarium market, or for consumption in restaurants. The fishermen often break apart the reef to look for hiding fish. The cyanide also kills large numbers of coral polyps, leaving large areas of the reef dead.

Reefs are also damaged when coral is taken for building material, jewelry, or aquarium ornaments.[6] Water pollution also results in damage. In addition, the recent warming of the oceans has caused areas of many reefs to turn white. Biologists are concerned that coral may be negatively impacted by further warming.

Changes in climatic conditions can affect the health of coral reefs, such as this one off the coast of Palau, in the Pacific.

Reasons for Hope

Threats to coral reefs are serious, but there is reason to hope that they will manage to survive. If we take steps toward coral reef conservation, it is likely that these tiny creatures, which have survived natural threats for millions of years, will be able to rebuild the damaged reefs that so many ocean animals and plants depend on.

[5] If an animal is **stunned**, it is confused or hurt and unable to move for a time.

[6] An **aquarium** is a building where sea animals are kept; an **ornament** is an attractive object that is put on display.

Reading Comprehension

A. Multiple Choice. Choose the correct answer for each question.

Gist
1. What is this passage mainly about?
    a. The use of coral in the construction industry.
    b. The wonder of coral reefs, and their threats.
    c. The kinds of fish found near coral reefs.
    d. The underwater world in general.

Did You Know?

Doctors sometimes use coral to replace missing pieces of bone in their patients.

Detail
2. Which statement about coral reefs is NOT true?
    a. They are an important source of fish.
    b. They are the world's most colorful places.
    c. They are usually found in deep ocean waters.
    d. They can be larger than structures made by people.

Detail
3. The material commonly called coral is made of _____.
    a. shells
    b. polyps
    c. reefs
    d. stone

Inference
4. Why does the author mention the price of reef fish in line 32?
    a. to excuse the fishermen who use illegal methods
    b. to explain why fishermen use cyanide
    c. to show why illegal fishing is attractive
    d. to make a connection to other factors damaging the reef

Main Idea
5. Which sentence best expresses the main idea of the final paragraph?
    a. Coral polyps and reefs are in little danger and don't really need our help.
    b. Coral polyps are strong, and with our help reefs will continue to survive.
    c. It's important to remember that coral polyps and reefs are very old.
    d. Coral reefs have protected coral polyps for millions of years without our help.

B. Completion. Complete the sentences about threats to coral reefs. Use no more than three words from the passage for each answer.

Threats to Coral Reefs
1. Blast fishermen try to kill as many _____.
2. Coral is taken for use as aquarium ornaments, jewelry, and _____.
3. After fishermen release _____ into the reef, sick but living fish are then collected.
4. Living fish are sold to restaurants for a lot of money or to _____.
5. Warming ocean temperatures have caused parts of some reefs to _____.

Vocabulary Practice

A. Definitions. Read the information below. Then match each word in red with its definition.

Not all coral is found in warm, shallow water. Some coral polyps can even survive without sunlight in the deep, cold waters at the bottom of the northern Pacific Ocean. But they are not safe from the method of fishing known as bottom trawling. Bottom trawlers pull heavy, weighted nets across the ocean floor. These nets have a very negative effect on deep sea coral. Though trying to catch fish, these nets destroy all the coral and the coral ecosystems in their way. The conservation of these ecosystems is important for the future of many of the ocean's plants and creatures. A new U.S. law prevents bottom trawling in over a million square kilometers of ocean off its Pacific coast. Keeping these ecosystems healthy is important for future generations of sea life, as well as for the people who will depend on that life.

▲ The heavy, weighted nets of bottom trawlers can cause great damage to the sea floor.

1. taking care of the environment _____
2. the opposite of *deep* _____
3. living things that are not plants _____
4. the opposite of *positive* _____
5. groups of living things of similar age _____

B. Words in Context. Complete each sentence with the best answer.

1. A source of a material is the place where it _____.
   a. is used   b. comes from
2. If a fish is consumed by someone, it is _____.
   a. eaten   b. cooked
3. A _____ is an example of jewelry.
   a. ring   b. dish
4. If water is polluted, it is probably _____ to drink.
   a. safe   b. unsafe
5. A brilliantly colored fish is _____ to see.
   a. easy   b. difficult

Word Partnership

Use **negative** with:
(*n.*) negative **effect**, negative **experience**, negative **image**, negative **attitude**, negative **thoughts**, negative **comment**, negative **response**

The Truth About Sharks

☐ Before You Read

A. Completion. Complete the information with the words and phrases from the box.

teeth	length	nets	dead things	a type of fish

Great White Shark Facts

Type: Like all sharks, great whites are **1.** _____.

Size: They are 4.6 to 6 meters in **2.** _____. (They can be longer than a bus!)

Weight: They can weigh up to 2,268 kilograms or more.

Jaws: They have up to 3,000 **3.** _____ in several rows.

Food: Their diet includes fish, seals, sea lions, small whales, and **4.** _____.

Threats: They are threatened by overfishing and accidental catching in **5.** _____.

Situation: Great whites are endangered.

B. Predict. What do you think is meant by "The Truth About Sharks?" Read the passage to check your ideas.

Shark Attack!

The jaws of a great white shark ► hold up to 3,000 razor-sharp teeth.

1   Craig Rogers was sitting on his surfboard,[1] scanning the distance for his next wave, when his board suddenly stopped moving. He looked down and was terrified to see a great white shark biting the front of his board. "I could have touched its eye with my elbow," says Craig. The shark had surfaced so quietly he hadn't heard a thing.

5   In his horror and confusion, he waved his arms and accidentally cut two of his fingers on the shark's teeth. He then slid off the opposite side of his surfboard into the water. Then, with Craig in the water and blood flowing from his fingers, the five-meter-long shark simply swam away, disappearing into the water below.

▲ Most people who are attacked by great white sharks—including this diver—survive to tell the tale. Researchers are unsure why sharks normally let humans escape.

Although sharks are often categorized as killers that
10 hunt and eat as many humans as they can, this is factually inaccurate. Sharks very rarely kill humans. A person has a greater chance of being struck by lightning[2] or drowning[3] in a bath than of being killed by a shark. Only 74 people have been reported killed by great whites in the last century. But
15 great white sharks can reach six meters in length and weigh 2,200 kilograms or more. With frightening jaws that can hold up to 3,000 teeth arranged in several rows, they could very easily kill and eat a helpless human in the water. Why is it, then, that most people survive attacks by great whites? Shark
20 researchers are trying to comprehend the reasons that allow people to escape without being eaten.

[1] A **surfboard** is a long narrow board used for surfing.
[2] **Lightning** is the very bright flashes of light in the sky that happen during rainstorms.
[3] When someone **drowns**, they die because they have gone under water and cannot breathe.

The most common explanation is that great whites don't see well. It has been thought that they mistake people for the seals or sea lions which make up a large part of their diet. There is reason to doubt this, however. Recent information shows that great whites can actually see very well. Also, when attacking seals, great whites shoot up to the surface and bite with great force. When approaching humans, however, they most often move in slowly and bite less hard. They soon discover that humans are not a high-fat meal. "They spit us out because we're too bony," says Aidan Martin, director of ReefQuest Center for Shark Research.

Shark researchers like Martin hypothesize that great whites are actually curious animals that like to investigate things. It's possible that they use their bite not only to kill and eat, but also to gather information. Although such an experience is unlucky for people like Craig Rogers, when sharks bite surfboards or other objects or people, they are likely just trying to learn what they are.

▲ When attacking seals, a great white shark shoots to the surface and bites with great force.

▲ Are great whites just curious animals, rather than fearless killers?

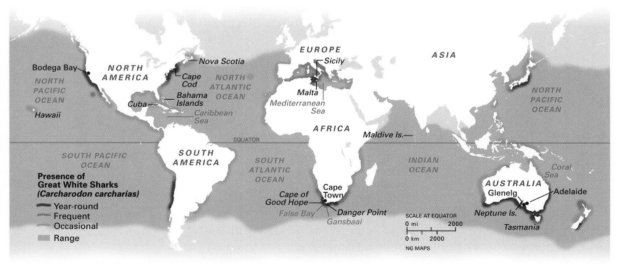

◄ Great whites are protected off Australia, the southern coast of Africa, and in several other seas around the world.

Presence of Great White Sharks (Carcharodon carcharias)
— Year-round
— Frequent
— Occasional
Range

Reading Comprehension

A. Multiple Choice. Choose the correct answer for each question.

Detail

1. After Craig Rogers fell into the water, the shark _____.
   a. bit his surfboard
   b. bit his fingers
   c. swam away
   d. attacked him

Detail

2. It is difficult for the author to understand why great whites _____.
   a. often let humans escape
   b. kill humans
   c. have so many teeth
   d. grow to six meters or more

> **Did You Know?**
>
> Great whites can sense even tiny amounts of blood in the water up to five kilometers away.

Reference

3. The word *their* in line 26 means _____.
   a. people's
   b. great whites'
   c. sea lions'
   d. seals'

Main Idea

4. What is the main idea of the third paragraph?
   a. Great whites eat low-fat, bony meals more slowly.
   b. Great whites see well enough to include seals, sea lions, and humans in their diet.
   c. We now know great whites don't mistake humans for other animals.
   d. There is reason to doubt that great whites see well enough to attack humans.

Vocabulary

5. Which of the following is closest in meaning to *make up* on line 25?
   a. create
   b. are
   c. increase
   e. depend upon

▲ A great white approaches cage divers off the Australian coast.

B. Fact or Theory? Which of these statements about great whites are facts (**F**) and which are theories (**T**)?

_____ **a.** Great whites can see well.
_____ **b.** Great whites are curious animals.
_____ **c.** Great whites bite to get information.
_____ **d.** Great whites eat seals and sea lions.
_____ **e.** Great whites vary the force of their bite.

Vocabulary Practice

A. Completion. Complete the information with words from the box.
One word is extra.

| bite | confusion | factual | arrange | inaccurate | horror |

In 1974, writer Peter Benchley wrote the famous novel *Jaws* on the subject of a killer shark that hunted humans around a small island. The next year, Steven Spielberg created the movie of the same name which gave audiences around the world a feeling of **1.** _____ towards sharks. While the movie was thrilling, it led to some **2.** _____ about the true nature of sharks. The behavior of the shark shown in *Jaws* is actually quite **3.** _____. The truth is that sharks very rarely **4.** _____ humans, even when given the opportunity. In his later life, Peter Benchley felt bad about spreading false information and worked to educate adults and children with **5.** _____ information about sharks.

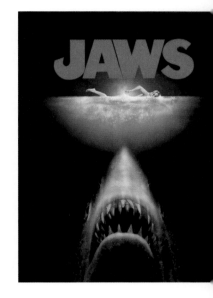

B. Completion. Complete the sentences using the correct form of words in the box.

| arrange | comprehend | hypothesize | categorize | gather |

1. Because sharks are seen as dangerous killers, it's difficult for most people to _____ that sharks are actually in danger from humans and need our protection.

2. Whale sharks, the largest sharks in the world, never bite or chew, although they have thousands of tiny teeth _____ in more than 300 rows.

3. Scientists _____ that the decline in the number of sharks may be related to overfishing.

4. Each year, great white sharks _____ off Cape Town to eat seals, which are plentiful in South Africa's water.

5. Hundreds of sharks have been _____ as endangered species by the International Union for Conservation of Nature.

> ## Word Link
> *in–* can be added to some words to form the opposite meaning, e.g., *in*accurate, *in*ability, *in*action

Swimming with Sharks

A. Preview. Look at the picture and answer the questions.

1. Would you pay money to dive[1] with sharks?
   a. yes   b. no

2. Do you think feeding sharks should be banned?[2]
   a. yes   b. no

3. Which animals do you think bite more people each year: dogs or sharks?
   a. dogs   b. sharks

▲ A group of tourists dive with sharks in the Bahamas.

[1] If you **dive**, you go under the surface of the sea using special breathing equipment.

[2] To **ban** something means to state officially that it must not be done, shown, or used.

B. Summarize. Watch the video, *Swimming with Sharks.* Then complete the summary below using the correct form of words from the box. Two words are extra.

bite	creatures	hypothesize	shallow
factual	inaccurate	comprehend	gather
negative	confuse	horror	consume

Many tourists go to places like Florida, Hawaii, and the Bahamas to dive with sharks. Of all the **1.** _____ in the sea, they are the most interesting to some people. Attracting sharks by feeding them used to be common, too. However, in 2002, there were a large number of shark attacks on humans. Many people felt **2.** _____ at these attacks, and they gave sharks a very **3.** _____ image. The practice of feeding sharks was made illegal in Florida and other places.

Nonetheless, the idea that sharks kill a lot of people is **4.** _____. Each year, snakes kill more people, and dogs attack more people, than do sharks. Most shark attacks are just one quick **5.** _____. The shark rarely tries to eat the person. Researchers also **6.** _____ that sharks sometimes **7.** _____ humans for the other types of animals they usually **8.** _____, such as seals or fish. Once the shark **9.** _____ that it has made a mistake, it leaves.

By swimming with sharks, people can get first-hand, **10.** _____ information about them, and perhaps can become less afraid of them.

C. Think About It.

1. Do you think shark tourism should be encouraged in places that have sharks? Why or why not?

2. Do you think it is important to protect the sea and the animals in it? If so, what can people do to help preserve it?

 To learn more about life in the ocean, visit elt.heinle.com/explorer

A. Crossword. Use the definitions below to complete the missing words.

Across

1. based on facts
5. to speak against; to show dislike or disapproval of something
6. put or built in a certain place
8. a hole in the side of a cliff or hill, or under the ground
11. to live in a place
13. to protect against damage over time
15. unprotected; uncovered
16. where something comes from, e.g., a river
17. to use your teeth to cut into something
18. opposite of positive
19. to be all around something

Down

2. easy and useful
3. to turn around a center
4. to allow; to let
7. to understand
8. a number of events that are repeated in the same order
9. a living thing
10. to pay no attention to
12. concerned with money and business
14. to move slowly downward in water or sand

B. Notes Completion. Scan the information on pages 88–89 to complete the notes.

Field Notes

Site: Great Barrier Reef

Location: Queensland, _____

Information:

- The world's largest structure made by _____ made up of _____ reefs
- It has over 400 types of _____ and 1,500 species of _____
- Some fish can change their _____ or sex, or _____ themselves to other fish
- Great Barrier Reef Marine Park was established in _____ to protect the reef
- Volunteers help to remove _____ and make people aware of harm caused by _____

Underwater Wonders

Site: **Great Barrier Reef**

Location: **Queensland, Australia**

Category: **Natural**

Status: **World Heritage Site since 1981**

Great Barrier Reef

Australia's Great Barrier Reef is in fact not one large reef, but a huge area with more than 2,800 smaller reefs. Distributed along 2,000 km (1,250 miles) of coastline, it is the largest structure in the world made by living things.

Over 400 types of coral, 1,500 species of fish, and approximately 4,000 types of **mollusks** reside in, on, and around the reef. Together, these creatures make up a complex, multi-layered world. The power source that gives energy to it all is the sun. Plants (mostly **algae**) derive energy from sunlight and turn it into food and building materials, which support all other life in the water.

Each year, about 800,000 visitors—from vacationing families to qualified scuba divers— come to view this remarkable world beneath the waves. Strict regulations control which sectors of the reef are open to tourists, with the result that 95% of sightseers visit just 5% of the reef. This policy enables visitors to enjoy the reef while at the same time preserving it for future generations.

▲ **Perfect Partnership**
A reef fish known as a "sweet-lips" has its skin and mouth cleaned by a wrasse. The sweetlips doesn't object to this process—the wrasse's cleaning helps to stop infection and disease.

▲ Surrounded by Fish
Divers such as Douglas Chadwick (left, with a potato cod) may find themselves surrounded by curious reef residents. "It's like breathing pure adventure down there," says Chadwick.

Why So Varied?

New fish species, some as brightly-colored as jewelry, are found every year at the Great Barrier Reef. Some species can change their colors to hide from an enemy that is threatening them, or to conveniently attach themselves to another fish for a quick ride. Others are able to change their sex as they grow older.

But why is the reef so varied and colorful? "The answer," says David Bellwood, a marine biologist, "is that we really don't know." It may have been due to a lucky combination of circumstances—the right amount of warm water, sunlight, and thousands of years of time. During the Ice Age sea levels dropped, exposing parts of the sea bottom and creating smaller, shallower seas. This enabled fish populations to develop into different species. Later, sea levels rose and the species mixed, creating the brilliant variety we see today.

▼ An airplane seems tiny as it flies across Australia's huge Great Barrier Reef—the world's largest structure made by living things.

Protecting the Reef

Great Barrier Reef Marine Park was established in 1975 to protect the reef against the negative effects of tourism and economic development. Today, people are permitted to fish in certain locations, but other areas are "no-take zones," or places only for research and conservation. Professional organizations are assisted by **volunteers** such as the Order of Underwater Coral Heroes, a group which helps to clean garbage from the reef and raises public awareness of the harm caused by pollution. The letters of the name —OUCH!—appealed to its co-creator, diving instructor Tony Fontes: "It lets us tell people that's how coral feels when you **drag** an **anchor** across it!"

Glossary

algae: a type of plant that grows in water
anchor: a heavy object that prevents a ship from moving
drag: to pull along the ground, with difficulty or effort
mollusk: a soft-bodied sea animal (snails, squids, etc.), usually enclosed in a shell
volunteer: a person or group that performs a service for no money

Water

A Global View

Earth is a watery planet. More than 70 percent of its surface is covered by salt water. This huge body of water includes Earth's four main oceans—the Pacific, Atlantic, Arctic, and Indian Oceans—as well as smaller features such as seas, **gulfs** (large areas of sea that extend a long way into surrounding land), and narrow water passages known as **channels**.

The ocean is always in motion. The spin of the Earth, together with wind and the amount of salt in the water, generates a system of **currents**, at the surface and deep in the ocean, called the **circulation** system. These currents constantly redistribute warm and cold water around the planet, influencing climate patterns and protecting Earth from extreme climate changes.

For humans and all other life on Earth, water is as important as air. But one in six people in the world do not have access to clean water. It is estimated that 9,000 people—mainly children—die every day from water-carried disease.

Ocean Circulation ▼

Warm surface water in the **tropics** (the areas just north and south of the equator) moves north and south, toward the **poles**. As it cools, it sinks and flows back to the equator. There, the water rises again, completing the cycle.

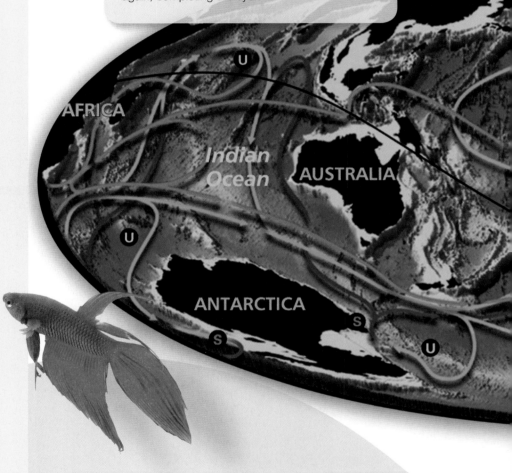

ASIA

AFRICA

Indian Ocean

AUSTRALIA

ANTARCTICA

Fresh Water

About two thirds of our planet is covered by water, but fresh water—needed for human survival, farming, and the environment—makes up only 2.5 percent of the Earth's total water. And of that amount, the majority is distributed as frozen **glaciers** or distributed underground as **groundwater**. Overall, less than 0.1 percent of the world's water is both fresh and accessible (readily available) for humans. As a result of environmental pollution and the demands of a growing population, water conservation is becoming an increasingly important issue in many parts of the world.

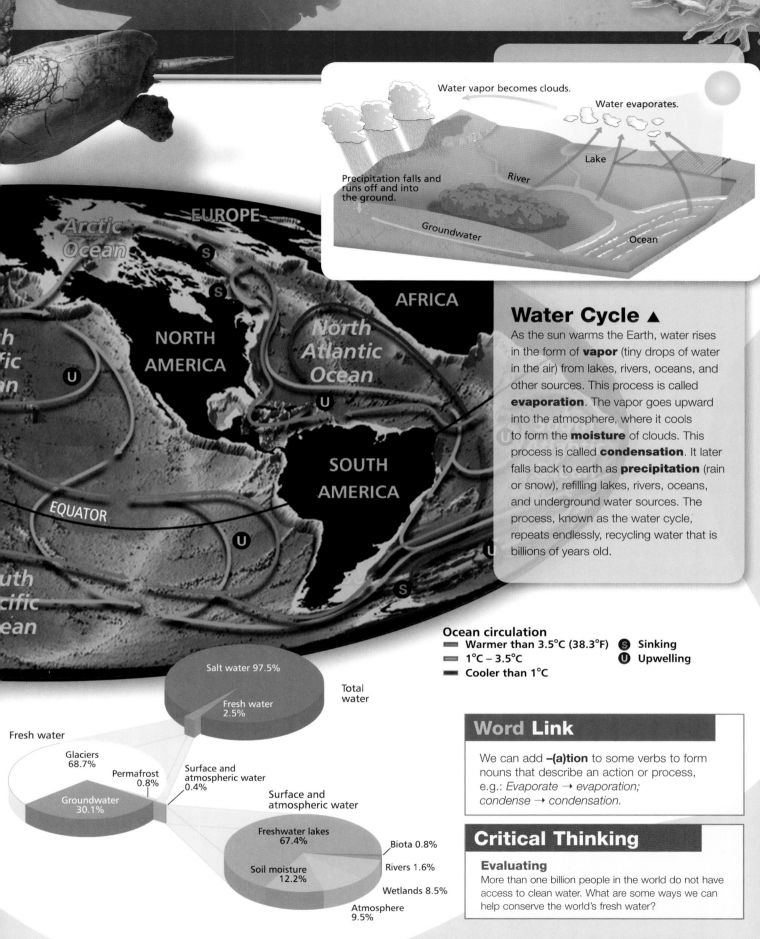

Water vapor becomes clouds.

Water evaporates.

Precipitation falls and runs off and into the ground.

River

Lake

Groundwater

Ocean

EUROPE

Arctic Ocean

AFRICA

NORTH AMERICA

North Atlantic Ocean

SOUTH AMERICA

EQUATOR

Water Cycle ▲

As the sun warms the Earth, water rises in the form of **vapor** (tiny drops of water in the air) from lakes, rivers, oceans, and other sources. This process is called **evaporation**. The vapor goes upward into the atmosphere, where it cools to form the **moisture** of clouds. This process is called **condensation**. It later falls back to earth as **precipitation** (rain or snow), refilling lakes, rivers, oceans, and underground water sources. The process, known as the water cycle, repeats endlessly, recycling water that is billions of years old.

Ocean circulation

▬ Warmer than 3.5°C (38.3°F) ⓈSinking
▬ 1°C – 3.5°C ⓊUpwelling
▬ Cooler than 1°C

Salt water 97.5%

Total water

Fresh water 2.5%

Fresh water

Glaciers 68.7%

Permafrost 0.8%

Surface and atmospheric water 0.4%

Groundwater 30.1%

Surface and atmospheric water

Freshwater lakes 67.4%

Biota 0.8%

Soil moisture 12.2%

Rivers 1.6%

Wetlands 8.5%

Atmosphere 9.5%

Word **Link**

We can add **–(a)tion** to some verbs to form nouns that describe an action or process, e.g.: *Evaporate → evaporation; condense → condensation.*

Critical Thinking

Evaluating

More than one billion people in the world do not have access to clean water. What are some ways we can help conserve the world's fresh water?

Vocabulary Building 2

A. Definitions. Use words in **bold** from pages 90–91 to complete the sentences.

1. A _____ is a large area of sea or ocean that is partly surrounded by land.
2. A _____ is a huge river of ice that moves slowly, often down a mountain.
3. A _____ is a steady, continuous, flowing movement of water or air.
4. A _____ is a passage along which water flows.
5. The Earth's _____ are found at opposite ends of the globe, at extreme north and south.
6. The _____ are the hottest parts of the Earth.
7. When water vapor condenses, it forms _____.

B. Word Link. We can add **–(a)tion** to certain verbs to form nouns that describe an action, state, or process. Complete each chart with the missing verb or noun form of the word. Then use the correct forms of the words to complete the passage.

Verb	Noun
1. circulate	*circulation*
2. combine	
3.	condensation
4. conserve	
5.	distribution
6. evaporate	

Verb	Noun
7.	generation
8. locate	
9.	pollution
10. precipitate	
11.	preservation
12. rotate	

When water from rivers and oceans _____, it rises into the air as vapor. As water vapor cools, it _____ to form clouds. _____ from clouds falls back to Earth, refilling rivers and other bodies of water. This endless _____ of water in its various forms is known as the water cycle. The process is vital for the survival of all life on Earth. The _____ of water across the planet is uneven, and many parts of the world do not have enough fresh water. Human activity can negatively affect the water cycle by causing _____— for example, by adding chemicals and throwing garbage to rivers and seas. _____ of fresh water is important so that future _____ have enough supply to meet their needs.

UNIT 7

Sweet Scents

WARM UP

Discuss these questions with a partner.

1. How many kinds of flowers can you name in English? Make a list.

2. Which flower do you think is the most beautiful? Which do you think has the best scent?

3. What are some of the ways in which people use flowers?

7A

The Business of Flowers

Before You Read

▲ Orchids growing in a greenhouse in Florida, U.S.A.

A long-stemmed rose in a vase ▶

A. Survey. Complete the survey about flowers. Then explain your answers to a partner.

	Yes	No
1. Do you prefer to **pick** flowers yourself to buying them from a **florist**?	❏	❏
2. Do you prefer **long-stemmed roses** to **orchids**?	❏	❏
3. Have you ever seen flowers growing in a **greenhouse**?	❏	❏
4. Have you ever bought flowers grown in another country?	❏	❏
5. Have you received flowers as a gift?	❏	❏
6. Do you think the appearance of a flower is more important than its **fragrance**?	❏	❏
7. Have you ever bought flowers to wear for a special event?	❏	❏
8. Do you always have **vases** of flowers around your house?	❏	❏
9. Have you ever bought flowers for no special reason?	❏	❏

B. Preview. Read the title, look at the pictures, and read the first and last sentences of each paragraph. Scan the reading for anything else that stands out. What is the reading about?

a. the condition of cut flowers around the world
b. the international business of cut flowers
c. technology in the cut flower business

▼ Two florists arrange their cut flowers for sale at a floating market in Valdivia, Chile.

The Flower Trade

1   When you purchase cut flowers from your local florist, do you think about where they came from? Common sense might tell you that they were grown close by, because cut flowers can't survive a very long trip. The reality, though, is that your cut flowers might come from places

5   like the Netherlands, Ecuador, or Kenya!

▲ Tulips brighten the countryside of the Netherlands, the world's leading exporter of cut flowers.

The Cut Flower Leader

Flowers can now travel long distances thanks to air freight[1] and high-tech cooling systems. Even the most delicate[2] orchid can be shipped to arrive fresh in most places on Earth. This allows

10   Americans, for example, to import some 70 percent of the cut flowers they buy.

The country that exports the most cut flowers is the Netherlands, which dominates the world cut flower trade. There, seven auction houses[3] handle about 60 percent of the world's cut flower exports.

15   Some auction houses are very large indeed—Aalsmeer, near Amsterdam, is an auction house in the sense that Tokyo is a city or Everest a mountain. Its scale is daunting. About 120 soccer fields would fill its main hangar, which holds five auction halls. Nineteen million cut flowers are sold here on an average day.

▲ The heart of the global flower trade, Aalsmeer processes 19 million flowers every day.

20   The Netherlands is also a world leader in developing new flower varieties. Dutch companies and the government invest a considerable amount of money in flower research. Their scientists try to find ways to lengthen a flower's vase life.[4] They also try to strengthen flowers to prevent them from being damaged while traveling on rough roads and to strengthen flowers'

25   natural fragrance.

[1] **Air freight** is the business of sending things from one place to another by airplane.

[2] If something is **delicate**, it is easy to harm, damage, or break and needs to be handled or treated carefully.

[3] **Auction houses** are companies that hold auctions, which are public sales where the price of an item is not yet decided and customers compete to buy it.

[4] **Vase life** means the amount of time a cut flower remains in good condition after being placed in a container with water.

The Benefits of Climate

Despite Holland's dominance of the flower market, there are many places with a better climate for growing flowers, and the climate of Ecuador is almost perfect. Mauricio Dàvalos is the man responsible for starting Ecuador's flower industry some 20 years ago. "Our biggest edge is nature," he claims. "Our roses are the best in the world." With predictable rainy periods and 12 hours of sunlight each day, Ecuador's roses are renowned for their large heads and long stems. The flower industry has brought employment opportunities and a stronger economy to regions of the country. "My family has TV now. There are radios. Some people have remodeled[5] their houses," says Yolanda Quishpe, 20, who picked roses for four years.

▲ A laborer in California, U.S.A., loads freshly cut flowers for shipment to a flower market.

In recent years, local growers in Ecuador have faced growing competition from greenhouses built by major international companies. Despite this, Dàvalos feels that the world cut flower trade is large enough to allow both high-tech international companies and smaller national growers to succeed—at least for the time being. But not all local growers are as optimistic. Lina Hale is an independent rose grower in the United States whose business is now under constant threat from cheaper imports from large companies. In the 1980s, her father predicted the situation would get worse: "I see a freight train coming down the track," he warned her, "and it's coming straight towards us."

[5] When a house is **remodeled**, large improvements and changes are made inside and/or outside.

Tuesday, 7 A.M.	**Tuesday, 1 P.M.**	**Wednesday, 6 A.M.**	**Wednesday, 8 P.M.**	**Thursday, 4 P.M.**	**Friday, 12 P.M.**
Roses are cut in the cool mountain air of Colombia and moved quickly to indoor cooling houses.	Workers categorize the roses based on length, shape, and color.	Roses are boxed and transported to Bogota Airport for the 3.5-hour flight to Miami.	Roses are checked by officials, then transported by truck, train, or plane.	Roses arrive at large markets in major U.S. cities, where they are purchased by flower sellers.	At journey's end, flowers are displayed in store windows. Once in a vase, most rose varieties last up to ten days.

Tuesday   Wednesday   Thursday   Friday

From Colombia to the U.S.A.
How a rose travels from mountain to vase in just three days.

Reading Comprehension

A. Multiple Choice. Choose the correct answer for each question.

Gist

1. What is this passage mainly about?
   a. the most commonly traded flowers
   b. the history of the flower trade
   c. recent developments in the flower trade
   d. the importance of climate to flower growing

Detail

2. Which of the following are mentioned as large investors in flower research?
   a. American companies and their government
   b. private companies and the Dutch government
   c. Mauricio Dàvalos and Ecuador's flower industry
   d. air freight and high-tech cooling companies

Did You Know?

The number one importer of cut flowers is Germany. Germans have a special passion for roses, most of which they buy from the Dutch.

Detail

3. What are researchers NOT mentioned as working on?
   a. changing the color of certain flowers
   b. lengthening a flower's vase life
   c. preventing flowers from being damaged while traveling
   d. strengthening a flower's fragrance

Vocabulary

4. The word *edge* on line 38 is closest in meaning to _____.
   a. end   c. angle
   b. advantage   d. difference

Inference

5. What did Lina Hale's father mean when he said "I see a freight train coming down the track" (line 54)?
   a. He could actually see a train.
   b. He knew his business would be threatened by cheap imports.
   c. The entire flower industry was under threat.
   d. He thought that customer interest in roses would decrease.

B. Classification. Match each description (**a–e**) with the country it describes.

   a. has an ideal climate for growing flowers
   b. dominates the flower export trade
   c. holds huge flower auctions
   d. has 12 hours of sunlight
   e. benefits economically from the flower trade

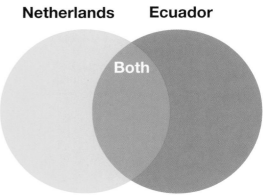

Netherlands   **Ecuador**

Both

Vocabulary Practice

A. Completion. Complete the information using the correct form of words in the box. One word is extra.

handle	export	prevent	considerable	trade	purchase

Tuesday, 7 A.M.	Roses are cut in the early morning, when the cool mountain air is cool. This helps to **1.** _____ their drying out.
Tuesday, 1 P.M.	Workers arrange the roses and put their stems in a special liquid to lengthen their vase life.
Wednesday, 6 A.M.	The roses are put in boxes and trucked to Bogotá Airport to be **2.** _____ to the United States.
Wednesday, 8 P.M.	The roses are imported to the city of Miami, a center for the flower **3.** _____ with the United States.
Thursday, 4 P.M.	The roses arrive at central markets in cities which **4.** _____ big orders from florists.
Friday, 12 P.M.	The roses are in florists' shops ready to be **5.** _____ by individual customers.

B. Words in Context. Complete each sentence with the best answer.

1. A company that dominates other companies _____.
a. beats them in business   b. assists them

2. If a company pays a considerable amount in taxes, it pays _____ amount.
a. a fairly high   b. a fairly low

3. Something that is claimed to be true is _____ true.
a. definitely   b. said to be

4. If you say a country is renowned for its flowers, you mean it is _____ for them.
a. envied   b. well known

5. A person seeking employment hopes to find _____.
a. a job   b. customers

Word Partnership

Use **handle** with:
(*n.*) handle **a job/a problem/a situation**;
handle **pressure/responsibility**
(*v.*) **difficult/easy/hard to** handle

Workers in Ecuador ▶
prepare long-stemmed
roses for export.

Marketing Perfume

Before You Read

A. Discussion. Read the information about perfume and cologne marketing. Then answer the questions about the bottles pictured below.

The marketing of perfumes and colognes is extremely important for sales. It can even be more important than the aroma itself. Imaginative marketing ideas, like the interesting bottles on this page, have helped to create excitement and hype around certain products. Marketers also create illusions of wealth, style, or well-being to attract customers.

1. Which bottle do you think is the most attractive? What do you like about it?
2. Which of these bottles do you think contain a fragrance for a man, for a woman, or for both?

B. Scan. How is basketball star Michael Jordan connected to the perfume and cologne industry? Scan the reading to find out, then tell a partner.

Perfume
A Promise in a Bottle

◀ Supermodel Christie Brinkley helps launch a new perfume which, she says, "celebrates real life rather than fantasy."

1   "Perfume," says expert perfumer Sophia Grojsman, "is a promise in a bottle." That promise might be reflected in a perfume's name: *Joy*, *Pleasures*, or *Beautiful*, for example.

5   Millions of dollars are spent on the marketing of a perfume, trying to get customers to connect luxury, attraction, or attitude to a fragrance.

▲ A young girl enjoys the smell of an Easter lily. Aromas such as flower scents have a powerful effect on our emotions and memory.

Even without all the marketing, fragrance has
10 power over our thoughts and emotions. Some scientists insist that memory and smell are especially closely linked. Certain aromas have the power to call up deep memories. Perfume makers are aware of this and use aromas that can touch us deeply.

The Power of Aromas

15 Of every ten new perfumes put on the market, perhaps only one will succeed. It's risky to try, as a company introducing a new fragrance can easily run through a budget of 20 million dollars. Profits, however, can be very high. One successful fragrance, *CK One* from designer Calvin Klein, made 250 million dollars in its first year.

In the perfume world, an essence is a material with its own special aroma. Some are
20 natural, derived from flowers, plants, or wood, for example. Others are synthetic[1] copies of rare or difficult-to-obtain essences. According to perfume authority Harry Frémont, a good fragrance "is a balance between naturals and synthetics. Naturals give richness and roundness; synthetics, backbone and sparkle."

Luxury scents ▶ are displayed like museum pieces at the Sephora perfume superstore in Paris.

Image and Marketing

25 Sephora is France's leading perfume store. In a store of shining stone, metal, and glass, famous perfumes are displayed and guarded like works of art in the nearby Louvre Museum.[2] Salespeople are dressed entirely in black, and each type of perfume is sold in a distinctly shaped bottle. In perfume sales, the emphasis is on presentation at least as much as on the product.

30 France's main competitor in the global perfume market is the United States, where image is all-important. The recent launch in the U.S. of one cologne for men, named after basketball star Michael Jordan, was preceded by a flood of TV commercials and talk show appearances by the player to create plenty of excitement and hype.

35 If you're confused about which perfume to buy, perfumer Annie Buzantian offers this advice: you really can't get an idea whether a perfume works or not until you wear it. "It's like the difference between a dress on the hanger and a dress on your body," says Buzantian. And Frémont adds, "Your first impression is often the right one."

[1] A man-made material that is not natural, but made with the help of science is **synthetic**.

[2] The **Louvre Museum** is a world-famous art museum located in Paris, France.

Women at a ▶ perfume company in New York test a new range of scents on a male co-worker. The team tests up to 2,000 scents every year.

☐ Reading Comprehension

A. Multiple Choice. Choose the correct answer for each question.

Main Idea
1. What is the main idea of the first paragraph?
   a. The perfume industry uses marketing to sell an idea.
   b. The name is the most important feature of a perfume.
   c. Perfume provides joy, pleasure, and beauty to customers.
   d. The perfume industry makes promises it can rarely keep.

Vocabulary
2. In line 16, the phrase *run through* is closest in meaning to _____.
   a. use completely   c. produce
   b. move into   d. earn

Detail
3. According to Harry Fremont, good fragrance is a balance between _____.
   a. flower and wood essences
   b. plant and man-made essences
   c. rare and difficult-to-obtain essences
   d. natural and man-made essences

▲ A civet

Detail
4. According to the author, in perfume sales, presentation is _____ the product.
   a. at least as important as
   b. much more important than
   c. nearly as important as
   d. not as important as

Inference
5. What is probably the main reason that Sephora's perfumes are so well guarded?
   a. Each bottle is worth over 1,000 dollars.
   b. The store has been robbed many times.
   c. It is a way to impress customers.
   d. French stores are normally well guarded.

Did You Know?

Civet, an essence derived from material taken from under the tails of civet cats, has long been valued as an ingredient in perfume.

B. Matching. Match the headings with the paragraph they describe.

1. Paragraph 2 ____   **a.** American-Style Marketing
2. Paragraph 3 ____   **b.** The Power of Fragrance
3. Paragraph 4 ____   **c.** Secret Ingredients
4. Paragraph 5 ____   **d.** High Risks, Great Rewards
5. Paragraph 6 ____   **e.** A Stylish Shop

Vocabulary Practice

A. Completion. Complete the information below with the correct form of words from the box. One word is extra.

distinct	emphasis	derived	obtain	essence	budget

In the history of perfume making, **1.** _____ derived from animals have only recently been replaced by man-made ones. For many years, a material known as *ambergris* was used in perfumes. Ambergris, which can be **2.** _____ by finding it floating on the ocean or lying on the sand on beaches, comes from inside certain whales. It has a very **3.** _____, long-lasting aroma. Ambergris is extremely valuable and too expensive for the **4.** _____of many perfume makers. Instead, man-made essences partly **5.** _____ from plants can give approximately the same aroma.

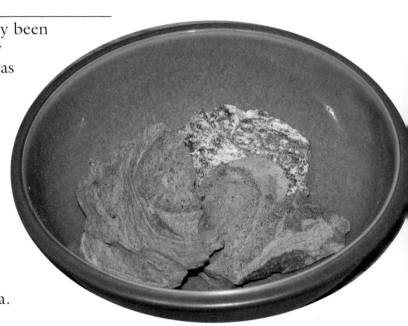

▲ Ambergris, produced by sperm whales, was once used in perfumes. Today, it has mostly been replaced by synthetic materials.

B. Words in Context. Complete each sentence with the best answer.

1. If you are asked to guard someone's jewelry, you should make sure _____.
   a. nobody steals it   b. you get a good price for it

2. An authority on perfume _____.
   a. owns a lot of it   b. knows a lot about it

3. Most commercials give information that _____.
   a. reflects well on a product   b. is negative about a product

4. If you are filled with joy, you are _____.
   a. very alarmed   b. very happy

5. When works of art are displayed at a museum, _____.
   a. everyone can enjoy them   b. they are kept out of sight

Word Partnership

Use *obtain* with:
(*adj.*) **able to** obtain, **difficult to** obtain, **easy to** obtain,
unable to obtain (*n.*) obtain **approval**, obtain **a copy**,
obtain **help**, obtain **information**, obtain **permission**

Madagascar Perfume

A. Preview. Read the information and discuss the questions with a partner.

Swiss chemists[1] are interested in the island of Madagascar off the east coast of Africa where they are looking for new scents[2] and flavors.[3]

1. What kinds of new scents and flavors do you think they might find there?
2. How do you think they will use those scents and flavors?

[1] A **chemist** is a scientist who studies the structure of materials and how they react with other materials.

[2] The **scent** of something is its smell.

[3] The **flavor** of something is its taste.

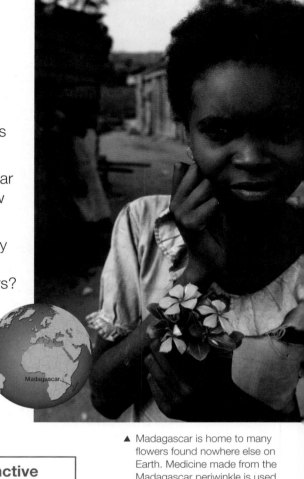

▲ Madagascar is home to many flowers found nowhere else on Earth. Medicine made from the Madagascar periwinkle is used to treat leukemia (a cancer of the blood).

B. Summarize. Watch the video, *Madagascar Perfume.* Then complete the summary below using the correct form of words from the box. Two words are extra.

authority	commercial	prevent	distinctive
essence	display	export	joy
obtain	purchase	renowned	considerable

The island of Madagascar has become an interesting place for Swiss chemists. Switzerland **1.** _____ products such as perfume, bath products, and juices to countries around the world. In order to **2.** _____ the flowers and fruits they use to produce the **3.** _____ that add flavors and scents to their products, they go to places like Madagascar.

In Madagascar, the chemists search for flowers or fruits that have a(n) **4.** _____ taste or smell—something that is unusual or different. In laboratory, the chemists spend a(n) **5.** _____ amount of time producing the essence of scent or flavor. Professor Roman Kaiser, who is **6.** _____ as a(n) **7.** _____ on the subject of scents and flavors, experienced a feeling of **8.** _____ when he created an essence that smelled very similar to the *Stephanotis* flower.

The next time you see a perfume **9.** _____ on TV or when you **10.** _____ a bottle of perfume for yourself or as a gift, remember the work of these Swiss chemists.

C. Think About It.

1. Do you think that the work done by chemists such as Willi Grab does is important? Why or why not?
2. What things do you own that have flavors or smells that come from flowers or fruits?

 To learn more about flowers and scents, visit elt.heinle.com/explorer

UNIT 8

Great Explorers

Discuss these questions with a partner.

1. Who are some great explorers from history?

2. What places remain to be explored today?

3. Would you like to be an explorer? Why, or why not?

▲ Yahya, a Tuareg guide, walks across sand dunes
in the Sahara Desert, Libya.

8A

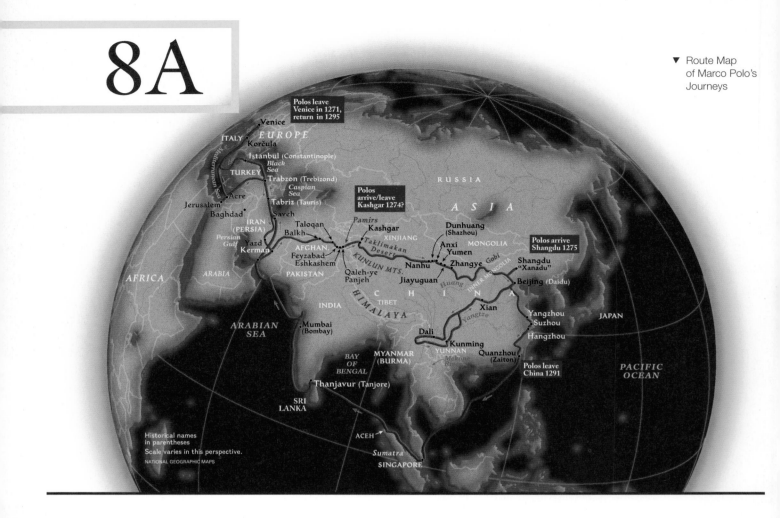

Marco Polo

☐ Before You Read

A. Discussion. Look at the map of Marco Polo's journey. Then answer the questions.
  1. Where did Marco Polo start and finish his trip? How many years did he travel for?
  2. What were some of the furthest places he reached during his travels?
  3. What other places did he visit? What do you know about these places?

B. Predict. Why do you think Marco Polo went on such a long journey? Read the passage to check your ideas.

MARCO POLO IN CHINA

▲ The sun rises at Jiayuguan, where a 14th-century tower on the Great Wall marks a traditional entryway to China. Marco Polo traveled eastward through these lands on his way to meet the Mongol lord Kublai Khan.

1　The Polos—Marco, his father Niccolò, and his uncle Maffeo—had been traveling for three-and-a-half years when they finally achieved their objective—a long-awaited meeting with the powerful Mongol leader, Kublai Khan. The historic event took place in 1275 at the Khan's luxurious summer capital[1] in Shangdu, in
5　what is now northern China. As he greeted his tired guests, Kublai Khan was surprisingly informal: "Welcome, gentlemen! Please stand up. How've you been? How was the trip?"

　　Marco Polo's trip had, in fact, started more than 9,000 kilometers (5,600 miles) away in Venice when he was just a teenager. His father and
10　uncle already knew Kublai Khan from a previous visit five years earlier, when they had spent a short time in Shangdu. On this second trip the Polos would stay for 17 years, making themselves useful to the Khan and undertaking various missions[2] and tasks for him. It is likely that the Khan considered it an honor[3] that Europeans—who were rare in China—had
15　made the extremely difficult journey, and he made good use of their skills and knowledge.

　　In the service of Kublai Khan, "the most powerful man in people and in lands and in treasure that ever was in the world," Marco was able to learn and experience many things that were new to Europeans. In his travel journal,
20　he described Kublai Khan's palace as the greatest he had ever seen. He admired the Khan's recently completed new capital, Daidu, whose streets were "so straight and so broad." The city was located in what is now the center of Beijing, and Kublai Khan's city planning can still be perceived in the straight, broad streets of China's modern capital.

▲ Marco Polo's 24-year trip opened up a world that had never before been described by any European.

[1] The **capital** of a country is the city where its government meets.

[2] A **mission** is an important task that people are given to do, especially one that involves traveling.

[3] Something that is an **honor** is special and desirable.

◄ Boats crowd an entrance to the Grand Canal near the Chinese port of Yangzhou. Marco wrote that he saw 15,000 boats a day sailing on the nearby Yangtze River.

▲ "Each day there come [to Daidu] . . . more than a thousand carts loaded with silk," wrote Marco. In some villages today, silk is still made the traditional way, by heating silkworm cocoons until they are soft enough to produce threads.

25 We learn from Marco Polo that, in the administration of his empire, Kublai Khan made use of a fast and simple message system. Horse riders spaced every 40 kilometers allowed messages to cover 500 kilometers a day. Marco also learned the secret of asbestos cloth, which is made from 30 a mineral and doesn't catch fire. Paper money also took him by surprise, as it was not yet in use in the West at that time. Homes were heated with "black stones… which burn like logs." Those stones were coal—unknown in most of Europe—and they were so plentiful that many people had a 35 hot bath three times a week.

Although the Khan did not want his visitors to leave, the Polos finally received permission to return home in 1292. Marco continued his observations on the ocean voyage by way of Sumatra and India. Upon his return, he completed 40 a book about his trip, full of details about his amazing cultural experiences. It was probably the greatest contribution of geographic information ever made to the West about the East.

Marco Polo completed ► his journal for "all people who wish to know . . . the different regions of the world." This valuable copy of his *Description of the World* is now kept in a library in Seville, Spain.

☐ Reading Comprehension

A. Multiple Choice. Choose the best answer for each question.

Gist
1. Who was Marco Polo?
   a. a young man from Venice
   b. a person who worked for Kublai Khan
   c. a writer of a book about his travels
   d. all of the above

> **Did You Know?**
>
> According to a biography by Christopher Columbus' son about his father, Marco Polo was an inspiration for Columbus' own voyages of discovery.

Detail
2. Where is Kublai Khan's influence still felt in Beijing today?
   a. in the food   c. in the universities
   b. in the streets   d. in the buildings

Detail
3. What allowed a message to cover 500 kilometers a day?
   a. runners   c. ships
   b. horse riders   d. asbestos

Inference
4. What does the use of asbestos cloth, paper money, and coal seem to tell us about the East and the West?
   a. The West had already improved on these areas of technology.
   b. The East had learned various technologies from the West.
   c. The West had forgotten these technologies still used in the East.
   d. The East was ahead of the West in some areas of technology.

Reference
5. In line 41, the word *it* refers to which noun?
   a. culture   c. book
   b. completion   d. contribution

B. Sequencing. Write the number of each event on the correct place on the timeline.

1. Marco begins working for Kublai Khan and traveling around China.
2. Niccolò and Maffeo depart to visit the Khan with Marco.
3. Niccolò and Maffeo visit the Khan without Marco.
4. Marco completes his book.
5. The three Polos leave China by ship.

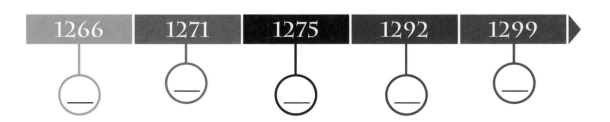

1266   1271   1275   1292   1299

Vocabulary Practice

▲ Tourists gather outsic the Doge's Palace, Venic Preserved as a museum, the building is much the same now as was in Marco Polo's day.

A. Completion. Complete the information with the correct form of words from the box. One word is extra.

objective	undertake	journal	palace	admire
perceive	administration	mineral	voyage	contribute

After surviving the dangers of the ocean **1.** _____ from China with the pleasant **2.** _____ of reaching his home city of Venice, more troubles were waiting for Marco Polo. Italy at that time was not united under one governmental **3.** _____, and the cities were often at war with each other. During fighting between Venice and the city of Genoa, Marco Polo was put in prison. It was there that he met the writer Rustichello. Rustichello **4.** _____ to Marco Polo's future fame by helping him to write down a(n) **5.** _____ of his world travels.

Nevertheless, some readers of Marco Polo's book have **6.** _____ that important details were left out, and they question the truth of the book. In order to check the truth of Marco Polo's journal, National Geographic photographer Michael Yamashita followed the path of Marco Polo. He **7.** _____ the task of checking the facts in the book and found that many are indeed true.

Nowadays, Marco Polo's doubters are few, and most people **8.** _____ him for his amazing travels. A sculpture honoring Marco Polo was placed in the Doge's **9.** _____ in Venice, one of the city's most beautiful buildings.

B. Definitions. Complete the definitions using the correct words from the box in **A**.

1. When you _____ a task or job, you start doing it and accept responsibility for it.

2. A(n) _____ is a long journey on a ship.

3. If you _____ someone or something, you like and respect them very much.

4. If you _____ something, you see, notice, or realize it, especially when it is not obvious.

5. A(n) _____ is a very large impressive house, especially the official home of a king, queen, or president.

6. _____ is all the activities associated with organizing and running a company or country.

7. Your _____ is what you are trying to achieve.

8. A(n) _____ is a notebook or diary.

9. If you _____ to something, you do something to help make it successful.

Word Partnership

Use **undertake** with:
(v.) undertake **an action**, undertake **a project**, undertake **a task**

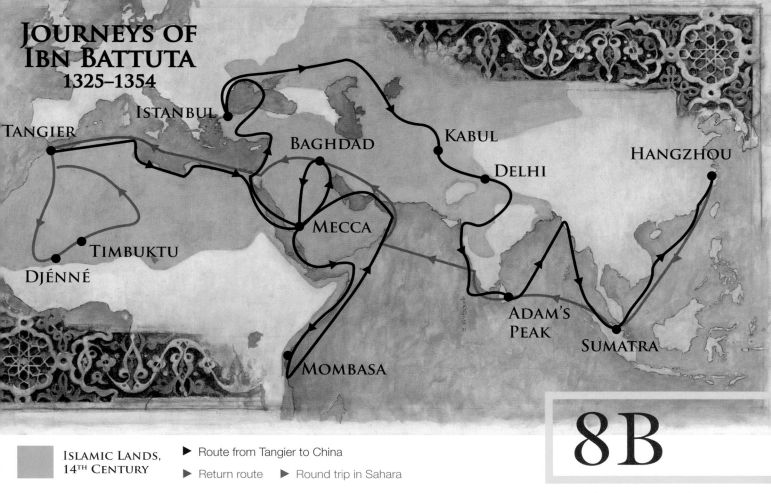

JOURNEYS OF IBN BATTUTA
1325–1354

TANGIER
ISTANBUL
BAGHDAD
KABUL
DELHI
HANGZHOU
MECCA
TIMBUKTU
DJÉNNÉ
MOMBASA
ADAM'S PEAK
SUMATRA

ISLAMIC LANDS, 14TH CENTURY
▶ Route from Tangier to China
▶ Return route ▶ Round trip in Sahara

8B

▲ Ibn Battuta spent several years in Mecca before heading on to India and beyond.

Prince of Travelers

☐ Before You Read

A. Discussion. Ibn Battuta was born in Tangier. He was a great traveler of the 14th century. Look at the map of his travels and try to guess the answers to these questions.

    1. Which religion did Ibn Battuta belong to?

    2. Which person traveled further, Ibn Battuta or Marco Polo?

    3. How many countries did Ibn Battuta visit?

    4. For how many years was Ibn Battuta traveling?

B. Scan. Now quickly read the first two paragraphs on page 112 to check your answers.

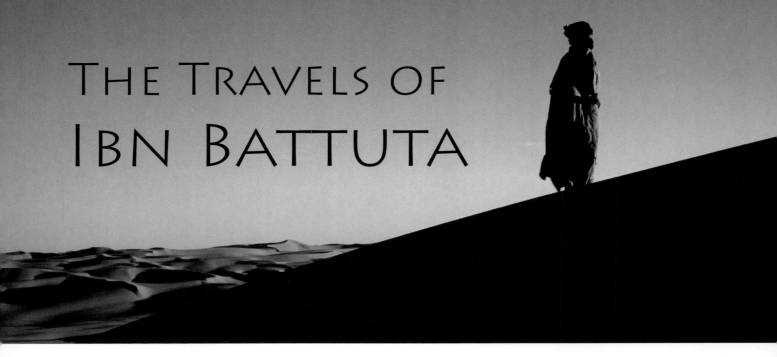

THE TRAVELS OF IBN BATTUTA

▲ During 30 years of traveling, Ibn Battuta visited the furthest edges of the Islamic world—from the deserts of North Africa to China and back.

▲ Ibn Battuta spent several years in Mecca before heading on to India and beyond.

1 "I left Tangier, my birthplace, the 13th of June 1325 with the intention of making the pilgrimage[1] [to Mecca]. . . . to leave all my friends both female and male, to abandon[2] my home as birds abandon
5 their nests." So begins an old manuscript[3] in a library in Paris—the travel journal of Ibn Battuta.

Almost two centuries before Columbus, this young Moroccan set off for Mecca, returning home three decades later as one of history's great travelers.
10 Driven by curiosity, he journeyed to remote corners of the Islamic world, traveling through 44 modern countries, three times as far as Marco Polo. Little celebrated in the West, his name is well known among Arabs. In his hometown of Tangier, a square,
15 a hotel, a café, a ferry boat, and even a hamburger are named after him.

Ibn Battuta stayed in Mecca as a student for several years, but the urge to travel soon took over. In one adventure, he traveled to India seeking profitable employment with the Sultan[4] of Delhi. On the way, he described his group
20 being attacked in the open country by 80 men on foot, and two horsemen: "we fought . . . killing one of their horsemen and about twelve of the foot soldiers. . . . I was hit by an arrow and my horse by another, but God in his grace preserved me. . . . We carried the heads of the slain[5] to the castle of Abu Bak'har . . . and suspended[6] them from the wall."

After losing his ships in a storm, Ibn Battuta continued on to the island of Ceylon (Sri Lanka), where he visited the mountain known as Adam's Peak: "When we climbed it, we saw the clouds below us, shutting out our view of its base."

25 In Delhi, the sultan gave him the position of judge, based on his prior study at Mecca. But the sultan had an unpredictable character, and Ibn Battuta looked for an opportunity to leave. When the sultan offered to finance a trip to China, he agreed. Ibn Battuta set off in three ships, but misfortune struck while he was still on the shore. A sudden storm grounded and broke up
30 two ships, scattering[7] treasure and drowning many people and horses. As he watched, the third ship, with all his belongings and slaves—one carrying his child—was carried out to sea and never heard from again.

After a lifetime of incredible adventures, Ibn Battuta was finally ordered by the Sultan of Morocco to return home
35 to share his wisdom with the world. Fortunately, he consented and wrote a book that has been translated into numerous languages, allowing people everywhere to read about his unparalleled journeys.

[1] A **pilgrimage** is a trip to a place of religious importance.

[2] If you **abandon** something, you leave it for a long time or forever.

[3] A writer's first version of a book, handwritten or typed, is called a **manuscript**.

[4] A **sultan** is a ruler in some Islamic countries.

[5] Someone who has been **slain** has been killed.

[6] If you **suspend** something from a high place, you hang it from that place.

[7] If things are **scattered**, they have been thrown or dropped so they are spread all over an area.

▲ Ibn Battuta met the Indian sultan at his luxurious palace in Delhi, surrounded by 200 soldiers, 60 horses, and 50 elephants covered in silk and gold. The Sultan sent him on a mission to China, which Ibn Battuta described as "the safest and best regulated of countries for a traveler."

◄ After reaching China and the East Indies (Indonesia), Ibn Battuta returned home to Morocco. He died in 1369 at the age of 64 near the town of Fez; the location of his burial site remains a mystery.

8B Prince of Travelers   **113**

Reading Comprehension

A. Multiple Choice. Choose the best answer for each question.

Gist

1. What is the passage mainly about?
   a. visitors to Mecca
   b. the adventures of Ibn Battuta
   c. Ibn Battuta's character
   d. Asian countries of the 14th century

Vocabulary

2. Which of the following is closest in meaning to *set off for* in line 8?
   a. left to go to   c. discussed
   b. arrived at   d. decided upon

Detail

3. The Sultan of Delhi gave Ibn Battuta a position of judge because _____.
   a. the sultan needed a translator
   b. Ibn Battuta had been a judge before
   c. Ibn Battuta had studied in Mecca
   d. Ibn Battuta had traveled to many countries

Inference

4. Which of the following would the writer of this passage most likely agree with?
   a. Ibn Battuta's journeys were very common for people of that time.
   b. Ibn Battuta's stories are probably not true.
   c. Ibn Battuta's journey was less important than Marco Polo's.
   d. Ibn Battuta should be more well known in the West today.

Detail

5. Why did Ibn Battuta finally return to his home?
   a. He was tired of traveling.
   b. He didn't have any more money.
   c. He feared the Sultan of Delhi.
   d. The Sultan of Morocco asked him to return.

Did You Know?

In Dubai there is a shopping mall named after Ibn Battuta. It has six sections named after areas of the world he visited.

B. True or False. Read the sentences below and circle **T** (true), **F** (false), or **NG** (not given in the passage).

	T	F	NG
1. Ibn Battuta left Tangier on his birthday.	T	F	NG
2. Ibn Battuta traveled further than Marco Polo.	T	F	NG
3. On his way to India, Ibn Battuta was injured.	T	F	NG
4. Ibn Battuta's trip from India to China was funded mainly by Ibn Battuta himself.	T	F	NG
5. Ibn Battuta had more than one child.	T	F	NG

Vocabulary Practice

A. Completion. Complete the information with the words in the box.
One word is extra.

unparalleled	remote	profitable	prior	consent	misfortune

The final journey of Ibn Battuta was to travel by caravan across the Sahara
Desert to the **1.** _____ land of Mali. Although he didn't
know much about the current king
of Mali, Ibn Battuta had heard
stories about a **2.** _____
king of Mali who had been the
grandfather of the current one. The
king's wonderful gifts to visitors
were **3.** _____, and
included large amounts of gold.
Ibn Battuta was probably thinking
that his trip to Mali would be a
4. _____ one, but
he was to be disappointed. It was
his **5.** _____ that the
current king, Mansa Sulayman, only
gave him a little bread, some meat,
and some vegetables. When he saw
his gift, Ibn Battuta could only laugh.

▲ Two Malian men wear their
traditional clothing.

B. Completion. Complete the sentences with the correct form
of the words in the box. One word is extra.

remote	consent	translator	unpredictable	finance	wisdom

1. Thanks to the work of many _____, the writings of Ibn Battuta
can be read in all major languages.

2. Weather is_____, so it is unwise to travel without checking
the forecast.

3. The king and queen of Spain _____ Christopher Columbus' voyage
to the New World.

4. Although he didn't want them to leave, Kublai Khan finally _____
to the Polos' request to return to Europe.

5. In order to make good decisions, it is necessary for a judge to
have _____.

Thesaurus **remote** Also look up: (adj.) faraway, distant

Crossing Antarctica

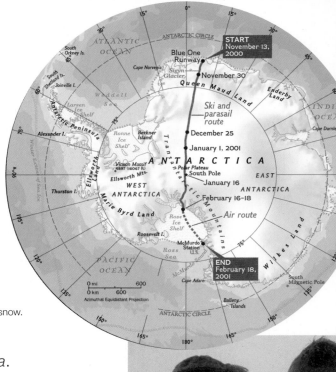

A. Preview. Finn Liv Arnesen and American Ann Bancroft, were the first women to cross the continent of Antarctica. How do you think they crossed it? Choose **a**, **b**, or **c**.

a. by dogsled

b. on skis[1]

c. by airplane

[1] **Skis** are long, flat, narrow pieces of wood you attach to boots to travel over snow.

B. Summarize. Watch the video, *Crossing Antarctica*. Then complete the summary below with the correct form of words from the box. Two words are extra.

admire	consent	contribution	remote
perceive	finance	journal	misfortunes
prior	unparalleled	unpredictable	voyage

Explorers Liv Arnesen and Ann Bancroft made an important
1. _____ to exploration history on Feb 11, 2001 when they crossed the **2.** _____ and icy continent of Antarctica on skis. The adventure was **3.** _____ because they were the first women to accomplish this feat. They think about their journey not only as one across an unknown land. They also **4.** _____ this remarkable feat as a
5. _____ of discovery inside themselves.

6. _____ to the trip, the two trained hard, skiing down rocky roads and pulling car tires behind them. Their training prepared them to successfully make progress over the dangerous land through **7.** _____ weather and winds. They did, however, meet with some **8.** _____ along the way as well.

During their adventure, through their Internet
9. _____, they communicated with the many people who **10.** _____ them. They have also written a book to share their adventure with the world. In the future, the two plan more exciting adventures.

▲ Explorers Ann Bancroft (left) and Liv Arnesen.

C. Think About It.

1. What are some of the challenges Arnesen and Bancroft faced?
2. What adventure would you like to go on? Why?

 To learn more about great explorers, visit elt.heinle.com/explorer

UNIT 9

Traditions and Rituals

WARM UP

Discuss these questions with a partner.

1. What is there about your culture that makes it unique?

2. What other cultures are you interested in? Why?

3. Do you have a favorite tradition?

▲ Candles light a cemetery to celebrate the Day of the Dead in Mexico.

117

9A

A Sporting Ritual

Japan

☐ Before You Read

A. Labeling. Read the sentences (**1–4**) and label the picture.
   1. A *sumo wrestler* aims to throw his opponent to the ground.
   2. Sumo matches take place in a circular earthen area known as a *dohyo.*
   3. Each sumo wrestler wears a belt called a *mawashi*.
   4. The wrestlers' hairstyle (called *chonmage)* dates back to 17th–century Japan.

B. Scan. You are going to read about sumo wrestling. Quickly scan the reading to answer the questions below. Then read again to check your answers.
   1. Apart from throwing their opponent, what else are sumo wrestlers allowed to do?
   2. What is the *mawashi* made of?
   3. Who used to wear the sumo wrestlers' hairstyle (*chonmage*)?
   4. How large is the *dohyo*?

GIANTS
of the Ring

▲ Two wrestlers come together at the center of a sumo ring.
Objective: to push the other wrestler over, or knock him out of the ring.

1　The two wrestlers[1] take some time to stare each other down. Then, suddenly, they
spring forward and impact with great force in the middle of the ring. Slapping,[2]
pushing, tripping, gripping the belt, and throwing the other wrestler are all allowed,
but punching[3] and kicking are not. The first person to be knocked down or pushed
5　out of the ring loses. The entire match usually lasts less than a minute.

The sport of sumo is Japan's traditional style of wrestling, and it is one of the
oldest organized sports on earth. Sumo matches were taking place in the seventh
century A.D. The basic elements of modern sumo began to fall into place in the
1680s, and the sport remains little changed since then.

10 Bigger Is Better

Sumo wrestlers are huge men by any standard. Their
average weight is 160 kilos, and there is no weight
restriction. The Hawaiian Salevaa Atisanoe, whose sumo
name is Konishiki, weighed over 280 kilos when he was
15　a successful wrestler. To achieve such impressive
dimensions, sumo wrestlers eat large quantities of *chankonabe*,
a Japanese stew whose ingredients include vegetables, chicken, fish, tofu,
or beef. In the ring, they wear, without shame, little more than a traditional
silk belt called a *mawashi*. Their hair is styled in a fashion popular with
20　17th-century samurai.[4]

▲ To achieve their
huge size, sumo
wrestlers follow
a regular daily
pattern: Practice.
Eat. Sleep.

[1] If you **wrestle** with someone, you fight them by forcing them into painful positions or throwing
them to the ground rather than by hitting them.

[2] If you **slap** someone, you hit them with an open hand.

[3] If you **punch** someone, you hit them with your closed hand, or fist.

[4] In Japanese history, the **samurai** were fighting men of the upper classes.

▲ As part of sumo's ritual, wrestlers throw a handful of purified salt before they step onto the clay.

▲ The sumo contest takes place beneath a shrine roof, illustrating sumo's close association with Japan's Shinto religion.

Ancient Traditions

Sumo matches are rich in tradition. The wrestling ring, called the *dohyo*, is exactly 4.55 meters across. Above it hangs a beautiful shrine[5] roof that illustrates sumo's close association with Japan's Shinto[6] religion. Wrestlers throw salt onto the ring before each match, a religious tradition believed to make the ground pure. Overseeing the fight is the *gyoji*, an official dressed in wonderful traditional clothes who closely watches and sometimes encourages the wrestlers.

Foreigners in Sumo

As Japan becomes more internationalized, so too does the world of sumo. Wrestlers from Mongolia, Korea, Russia, the United States, Argentina, and other countries have taken their turn in the ring. It's not surprising that so many people are entering the sport, since professional sumo wrestlers enjoy many benefits. Top wrestlers are national heroes and can earn more than one million dollars annually; some have even married movie stars.

Foreign wrestlers once found it difficult to advance in sumo. Konishiki once complained to the press, "If I were Japanese, I'd be a grand champion now." But since then, four wrestlers of foreign origin have become grand champions or *yokozuna*, the top level of sumo wrestler. Few other sports have been so successful at keeping their traditional roots while still appealing to a 21st-century audience. For this reason, the ancient and the modern will continue to meet in the sumo ring.

[5] A **shrine** is a religious place, often for a holy person or thing.
[6] **Shinto** is a religion of Japan.

◄ Top-level sumo wrestlers average 160 kilos (350 pounds); the heaviest can reach 280 kilos (600 pounds).

☐ Reading Comprehension

A. Multiple Choice. Choose the best answer for each question.

Detail

1. According to the passage, when were the earliest sumo matches taking place?
   a. in the seventh century
   b. in the 1680s
   c. in the 17th century
   d. before recorded history

Did You Know?

The heaviest ever sumo wrestler was Konishiki. He retired in 1997, but during his career he weighed as much as 275 kilograms.

Vocabulary

2. The word *standard* in line 11 is closest in meaning to _____.
   a. imagination
   b. measure
   c. name
   d. time

Detail

3. Which of the following is NOT allowed in a sumo match?
   a. throwing
   b. gripping the belt
   c. slapping
   d. punching

Reference

4. In line 24, what does *it* refer to?
   a. the ring
   b. Shinto religion
   c. the shrine
   d. the roof

Detail

5. How is the sumo world dealing with internationalization?
   a. It plans to allow it in the future.
   b. It accepts it.
   c. It is surprised by it.
   d. It doesn't allow it.

B. Matching. What is the main idea of each paragraph in the reading? Match a heading (**a–e**) with the correct paragraph (**1–5**).

_____ Paragraph 1   **a.** Religious Connections
_____ Paragraph 2   **b.** Fighting Methods
_____ Paragraph 3   **c.** Foreign Fighters
_____ Paragraph 4   **d.** The Look of the Wrestlers
_____ Paragraph 5   **e.** A Long History

Vocabulary Practice

A. Completion. Complete the sentences below using the correct form of the words in red.

The origin of sumo in Japan is older than recorded history. It wasn't until the Edo Period of Japanese history (1603–1867) that the sport began to look like the sumo we know today. During the Edo Period, the government kept a strong grip on the country, and travel in and out of Japan was very restricted. During the Meiji Period of Japanese history (1868–1912), the country opened up and began to take its first steps toward internationalization. Some people began to wear western style clothes and even had a sense of shame about Japanese–style clothes, but it was decided to keep the traditional clothes of sumo unchanged.

▲ Traditional Japanese clothing is still occasionally worn today, particularly at special events, such as weddings.

1. At the World Baseball Classic teams from 16 different countries play each other—a good example of the sport's move toward _____.

2. Sumo wrestlers are allowed to _____ the other wrestler's *mawashi* in order to throw them out of the ring.

3. The _____ of the sport of wrestling isn't known, but it is older than recorded history.

4. Although many drugs are illegal at the Olympics, athletes are not _____ in the amount of coffee they drink.

5. In 1919, residents of Chicago felt great _____ when it was learned that their baseball team had accepted money to purposely lose the national championship.

B. Words in Context. Complete each sentence with the best answer.

1. It is possible to illustrate an idea by _____.
   a. giving an example of it   b. showing it isn't true

2. Water that is pure is _____.
   a. clean and clear   b. mixed with other things

3. If an object from space impacts the earth, it _____.
   a. goes past it   b. hits it

4. A sports hero is a person who is _____ by many people.
   a. admired   b. forgotten

5. The dimensions of the painting were _____.
   a. two meters by three meters   b. bright and colorful

> **Word Partnership**
>
> Use **impact** with:
> **historical** impact, **important** impact, **make an** impact

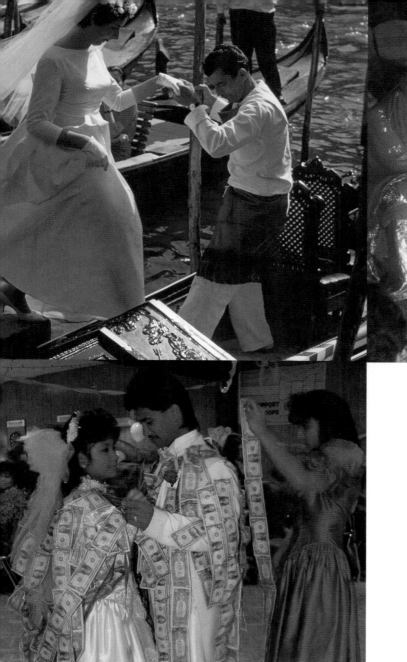

9B

Marriage Traditions

▲ In the presence of wedding guests, a bride and groom, covered in dollar notes, celebrate the start of their new life together on Kodiak Island in Alaska.

(*top left*) A bride receives a helping hand as she steps from a gondola in Venice, Italy. In Western traditions, a white wedding dress symbolizes purity, as does the wearing of a bridal veil.

(*top right*) Dressed in richly colored clothing, a man and woman sit respectfully as traditional marriage rites are performed at their wedding ceremony in Rajasthan, India.

A. Discussion. Look at the photos and captions. How are the weddings similar? How are they different? How do they compare with wedding traditions in your country?

B. Skim for the Main Idea. On the next page, look at the title, photos, and captions. What is this reading mainly about? Circle **a, b,** or **c.** Then read the passage to check your answer.

a. A famous African bride

b. A traditional wedding

c. Traditional desert clothing

BRIDE OF THE SAHARA

▲ On the first day of her wedding celebration, relatives and other women rub a scented cream, containing fine black sand, through Assalama's hair.

1　The Tuareg bride, Assalama, sits silently as female relatives and helpers make sure that every hair is perfect for the first day of her wedding
5　celebration. Such attention is new for the bride, who is only 15 years old and who has spent most of her time tending her mother's goats and sheep. The Tuareg are nomads,[1] and
10　it was only by chance that she was reunited with her 25-year-old cousin[2] Mohamed a month earlier. Just back from five years working in Libya, Mohamed spotted Assalama as she
15　drew water from a well. "I knew from that moment that I wanted to marry her," he says. Wasting no time, he asked for her hand, she accepted, their families approved,
20　and wedding plans began.

Following Tuareg traditions, the marriage rite is performed at a nearby mosque[3] in the presence of only the couple's parents. Assalama and Mohamed are absent. A few days later, the time for the celebration approaches, and guests begin to arrive. For a week, some 500 guests enjoy camel races, sing, and eat rice, dates, and roasted meat
25　in tents under the Saharan stars.

▲ Henna, a reddish-brown coloring used on the feet and hands, is a traditional symbol of purity in North Africa.

Mohamed wears an indigo *tagelmust*, a cloth that wraps his head and face. The rich color, which rubs off onto the skin,
30　earned these once fierce[4] Saharan warriors[5] the title "blue men of the desert." For the Tuareg, the *tagelmust* is more than just clothing that keeps out the desert
35　sand and sun; it demonstrates respect and is thought to keep evil[6] creatures known as *jinns* away, as is henna, a reddish-brown coloring used on Mohamed's feet. Henna
40　is also a symbol of purity, and is reserved for a man's first marriage.

At the celebration, a tent called an *ehan*
is prepared for Assalama and Mohamed.
Women take down and put up the tent
45 every day of the celebration, making it slightly
larger each time to symbolize the progress of
the celebration and of the couple's relationship.
Assalama stays inside the tent during the whole
celebration, only showing her face or speaking to
50 Mohamed, her best friend, her mother, and one
special helper. During the celebration, neither
Assalama nor Mohamed is ever left alone for fear
they might be harmed by jealous jinns.

As the celebration ends, the couple prepares
55 to spend the first year of their marriage with
Assalama's family. Mohamed will offer
displays of respect to his in-laws, working hard
to win their approval. Once he does that, he will
take his bride back to his camp and start his
60 nomad's caravan moving again.

[1] **Nomads** are people who travel from place to place rather than living in one place all the time.

[2] Your **cousin** is the child of your uncle or aunt.

[3] A **mosque** is a place where Moslems go to worship.

[4] A **fierce** fighter attacks with great bravery and energy.

[5] A **warrior** is a fighter or a soldier, usually of past times, who was very brave and experienced in fighting.

[6] If you describe someone as **evil**, you think they are morally very bad and cause harm to other people.

▲ An unmarried Tuareg woman wears her traditional indigo headdress to the wedding.

▼ A Tuareg camel caravan crossing the Sahara desert

▼ A view of the Grand Mosque in the desert town of Agadez, the largest Tuareg town in Africa

☐ Reading Comprehension

A. Multiple Choice. Choose the best answer for each question.

Gist   **1.** What is the passage mainly about?
    a. the marriage difficulties of a young Tuareg couple
    b. the changing wedding customs of the Tuareg people
    c. the love story of two Tuareg cousins
    d. a description of the marriage of a Tuareg couple

Detail   **2.** During their actual marriage ceremony, Assalama and Mohamed _____.
    a. were not present
    b. showed respect to their parents
    c. wore traditional Tuareg clothing
    d. visited a nearby mosque

Inference   **3.** Henna would NOT be used on Mohamed's feet if _____.
    a. he were not wearing a *tagelmust*
    b. he were marrying a cousin
    c. he was thought to be very pure
    d. he had been married before

Detail   **4.** Why do women make the tent slightly larger each time?
    a. so Assalama's friend, mother, and helper can enter
    b. to show the progress of the couple's relationship
    c. because the celebration increases in size
    d. to keep jealous *jinns* away

> **Did You Know?**
>
> Camels have been known to survive 50 days without water, which causes them to lose up to a third of their body weight. In order to live, they can drink up to 150 liters of water at a time!

Reference   **5.** The word *that* on line 58 means _____.
    a. returning to his camp
    b. starting his caravan moving again
    c. living for a year with Assalama's parents
    d. finishing the wedding celebration

B. Matching. Match the words (**1–5**) with their significance in a Tuareg marriage (**a–e**).

____ **1.** tagelmust   **a.** where the actual marriage ceremony takes place
____ **2.** henna   **b.** clothing that is thought to keep evil creatures away
____ **3.** ehan   **c.** threatens to disturb the couple's happiness
____ **4.** mosque   **d.** houses the couple during the wedding ceremony
____ **5.** jinn   **e.** coloring used on Mohamed's feet

Vocabulary Practice

A. Completion. Complete the paragraphs below using the correct form of the words in the box. Two words are extra.

symbol	jealous	reserved	reunite	wrap
nearby	wedding	camp	demonstrate	tent

Like the Tuareg people, the Wodaabe are another nomadic African people who live in simple, light **1.** _____ that are arranged in **2.** _____ which they move from place to place. The Wodaabe love having visitors, and a special place in their camp is **3.** _____ for guests. The Wodaabe use the **4.** _____ of "birds in the bush" to describe themselves. This image **5.** _____ the constant motion of the lives of the Wodaabe, never staying in one place.

▲ Beauty is very important to Wodaabe men.

The two most important Wodaabe celebrations have to do with love. The *geerewol* ceremony is a time when young women have a chance to choose the man they will marry at a unique beauty contest. Beauty is very important in Wodaabe society, and indeed they consider themselves to be the most beautiful people in the world. In the contest, Wodaabe men, their heads **6.** _____ in attractive turbans, present themselves publicly, hoping to attract a woman to marry.

At the yearly *worso* celebration, thousands of Wodaabe families **7.** _____ to celebrate the past year's **8.** _____ of new couples and the new babies they have brought into the world.

B. Completion. Complete the sentences below using the correct form of the words in the box in **A**.

1. Something that is a(n) _____ of something seems to represent it because it is very typical of it.

2. If something is _____ for a particular person or purpose, it is kept specially for that person or purpose.

3. A(n) _____ is a small, light shelter made of cloth or other material, held up by poles and ropes.

4. When you _____ something, you fold paper or cloth tightly around it.

5. A(n) _____ is a marriage ceremony, and the party or special meal that often takes place after the ceremony.

6. If people are _____, they meet each other again after they have been separated for some time.

7. To _____ a fact means to make it clear to people.

8. A(n) _____ is a place where people live or stay in tents.

Word Link

Re- is added to verbs and nouns to make new verbs and nouns that refer to repeating an action or process. For example, *re-read* means *read again,* and someone's *re-election* is their being elected again.

Nubian Wedding

A. Preview. You will hear these words in the video. Match each word with its definition.

1. incense ___ **a.** A long, thin piece of material used for hitting people or animals

2. whip ___ **b.** A musical instrument made of skin stretched over a round frame

3. sword ___ **c.** A substance burned for its sweet smell, often as a part of a ceremony

4. drum ___ **d.** A weapon with a handle and long, sharp blade

▲ A Nubian man dances at a religious festival in El Umbarakab, Egypt.

B. Summarize. Watch the video, *Nubian Wedding*. Then complete the summary below using the correct form of words from the box. Two words are extra.

grip	impact	jealous	nearby
origin	purity	restrict	illustrate
reunite	symbol	wedding	wrap

The Nubian people of Egypt have a(n) **1.** _____ ceremony that lasts for one week. The air is perfumed with incense, and drums are played. Sharif, a Nubian groom, was **2.** _____ with the bride he chose two years before and hadn't seen since. The bride, Abeer, is painted in henna, a(n) **3.** _____ of her **4.** _____.

The **5.** _____ lands of the Nubian people were on the banks of the Nile river, but they were **6.** _____ from living there by the Egyptian government, who needed the land for a dam. Mohammed Nour explained the negative **7.** _____ of moving on the Nubian culture, such as the loss of traditions and language.

Nubian means gold, and the bride is **8.** _____ in gold jewelry. On the final night of the ceremony, after a meal, the groom **9.** _____ a sword in one hand and a whip in the other, and then leads neighbors through the **10.** _____ streets.

C. Think About It.

1. What are some examples of Nubian customs?
2. What other unusual wedding customs do you know?

 To learn more about traditions and rituals around the world, visit elt.heinle.com/explorer

A. Crossword. Use the definitions below to complete the missing words.

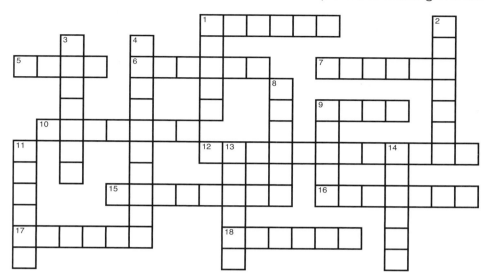

Across

1. something that represents something else
5. completely clean; not mixed with anything else
6. to hit forcefully, or to affect strongly
7. to get
9. to hold strongly onto something with your hand
10. wanting what someone else has
12. having no equal
15. to buy
16. to show (something); to put in a place where people can see
17. far away and difficult to get to
18. money available for something

Down

1. a feeling from doing something wrong or embarrassing
2. to provide money for a project or a purchase
3. to stop from doing
4. something unpleasant or unlucky that happens
8. a long journey
9. to watch and protect
11. to like and respect
13. only a short distance away
14. to send to another country

B. Notes Completion. Scan the information on pages 130–131 to complete the notes.

Field Notes

Site: Old Towns of Djénné and Timbuktu

Location: _____, West Africa

Information:

- Located between coastal forests and the _____
- 500 years ago, both cities were famous centers of culture and _____
- Djénné has over _____ homes made of _____, which are repaired by master _____
- Djénné's famous Great _____ is a copy of a 13th-century building
- Some 15th-century Europeans believed Timbuktu was made of _____
- Timbuktu is now famous for its collection of 100,000 _____

Sites: **Old Towns of Djénné and Timbuktu**

Location: **Mali**

Category: **Cultural**

Status: **World Heritage Site since 1988**

"Djénné of the future is Djénné of the past."

Thoukiri Samanaye, Djénné holy man

▲ Djénné's master masons are assisted by both young and old. Repaired regularly, the town's houses will last for generations into the future.

Five hundred years ago, the West African towns of Djénné and Timbuktu were renowned centers of culture and commerce. Located between the Sahara Desert and coastal forests, their vibrant marketplaces were filled with traders from distant lands who sold and purchased profitable goods like salt and gold.

Djénné and Timbuktu have another connection to the past that visitors come to admire: their unique mud houses and religious buildings. Today, Timbuktu's great mud mosques are distinctive symbols of Mali's "Golden Age," while Djénné has over 2,000 traditional mud **brick** homes that are centuries old but still lived in.

The task of maintaining these beautiful buildings is the life-work of Djénné's famous **masons**. Every year, seasonal floods and rain damage the houses, and the masons have to repair them to prevent them from **crumbling**. Each mason repairs the homes originally built by his ancestors, using skills passed down from father to son over hundreds of years.

Glossary

brick: a clay block used for building
crumbling: breaking up into small pieces
exotic: unusual and interesting
mason: a builder who works with stone or brick
the Koran: the holy book of Islam

The Great Mosque

When Djénné's rulers converted to Islam, they destroyed their palace and built a mosque instead. Today, the city's masons still use the teachings of **the Koran** to bless the homes they build, to protect each home from misfortune. Like their houses, the town's mosques are repaired regularly, using only water from a nearby river, clay from surrounding areas, and centuries of knowledge.

▲ The Great Mosque of Djénné is a copy of a building originally constructed in the 13th century.

A Golden City?

Long admired as a powerful trading center, Timbuktu became so famous for its wealth that 15th century Europeans claimed it must be made of gold. In fact, like Djénné, Timbuktu is made mostly of mud. Today, its real treasure is its collection of 100,000 ancient books, preserved and guarded by the town's families and the University of Sankore. Muslim scholars from the university helped to spread Islamic teachings across West Africa, making a considerable contribution to the internationalization of Islam.

◄ Timbuktu has long been a destination for explorers, including Ibn Battuta, who arrived in 1352. Even today, people still use the word "Timbuktu" to mean an exotic and remote place.

Trade

A Global View

Look at the labels on your television, your shirt, or your food. These are all evidence of the way in which the world is becoming increasingly interlinked. No single country has everything that it needs, so each country must exchange, or **trade**, with others. This results in a world of global economic interdependence—a commercial exchange between **"producers"** (those who produce or manufacture goods) and **"consumers"** (those who purchase or use the goods).

For some countries, international trade contributes more than half their national income. The trading system involves the exchange of **goods** (objects for trading) and **services** (skills or activities that people are paid to do). International trade enables countries to **export** the goods and services they are best at producing and to **import** those that are best produced abroad.

The greatest amount of trade occurs among the richest countries, which mainly exchange goods such as automobiles and luxury items. Trade also flows between higher- and lower-income regions: richer countries typically provide more complex goods, like electronic equipment, while low-income countries provide primary goods, like minerals.

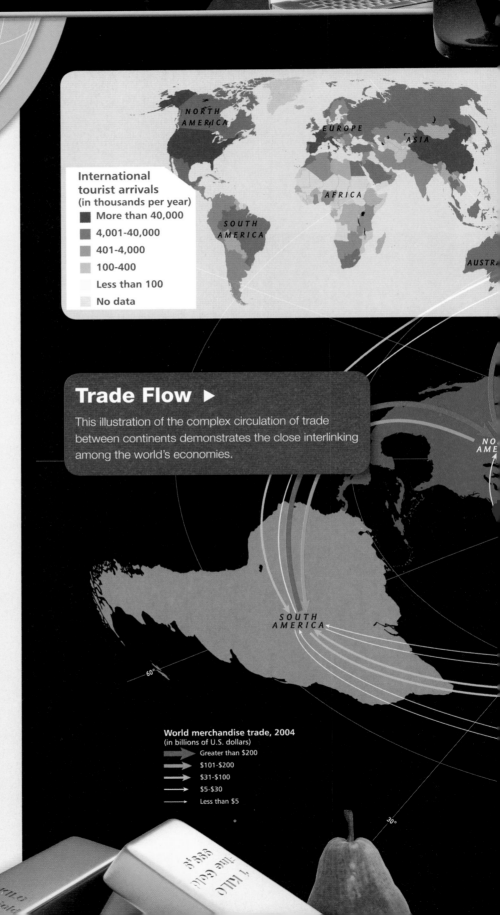

International tourist arrivals
(in thousands per year)

- More than 40,000
- 4,001-40,000
- 401-4,000
- 100-400
- Less than 100
- No data

NORTH AMERICA
EUROPE
ASIA
AFRICA
SOUTH AMERICA
AUSTRA

Trade Flow ▶

This illustration of the complex circulation of trade between continents demonstrates the close interlinking among the world's economies.

NO
AME

SOUTH AMERICA

World merchandise trade, 2004
(in billions of U.S. dollars)

- Greater than $200
- $101-$200
- $31-$100
- $5-$30
- Less than $5

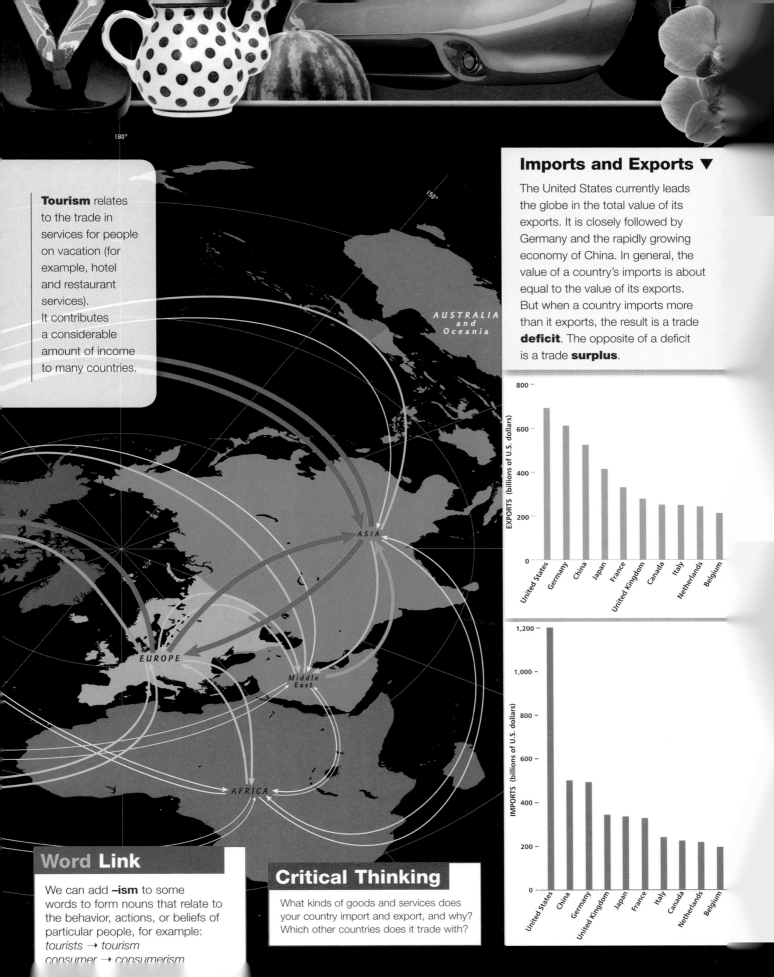

Tourism relates to the trade in services for people on vacation (for example, hotel and restaurant services). It contributes a considerable amount of income to many countries.

Imports and Exports ▼

The United States currently leads the globe in the total value of its exports. It is closely followed by Germany and the rapidly growing economy of China. In general, the value of a country's imports is about equal to the value of its exports. But when a country imports more than it exports, the result is a trade **deficit**. The opposite of a deficit is a trade **surplus**.

Word Link

We can add **–ism** to some words to form nouns that relate to the behavior, actions, or beliefs of particular people, for example:
tourists → tourism
consumer → consumerism

Critical Thinking

What kinds of goods and services does your country import and export, and why? Which other countries does it trade with?

A. Completion. Use the correct form of words in **bold** from pages 132–133 to complete the passage.

To _____ is to exchange something with another person or country. The global trading system is made up of exchanges between _____ (the people and countries who create particular _____ and services), and _____ (the people and countries who buy them).

When a country _____ a particular item, it sends it overseas to be sold in other countries. If a country sells more goods and services than it brings in from other countries, the result is a trade _____.

B. Word Link. We can add **inter-** to some words to refer to things that move, exist, or happen between two or more people or things. Complete the sentences below using the correct form of words from the box. Use a dictionary to help you. One word is extra.

interpret	Internet	interview	interact
intercontinental	interdependent	interchange	

1. The growth in global tourism has been driven by the availability of _____ flights.
2. An increasing number of tourists now use the _____ to make flight and hotel bookings.
3. Countries that are _____ rely on each other for trade.
4. The global trading system involves _____ of goods and services across international borders.
5. An economist is someone who is trained to _____ economic data.
6. Business newspapers and magazines often contain _____ with famous business leaders.

UNIT 10

Global Warming

Discuss these questions with a partner.

1. Are people worried about global warming where you live?

2. What changes could occur if the world gets warmer in the future?

3. What can individual people do about global warming? What can governments do?

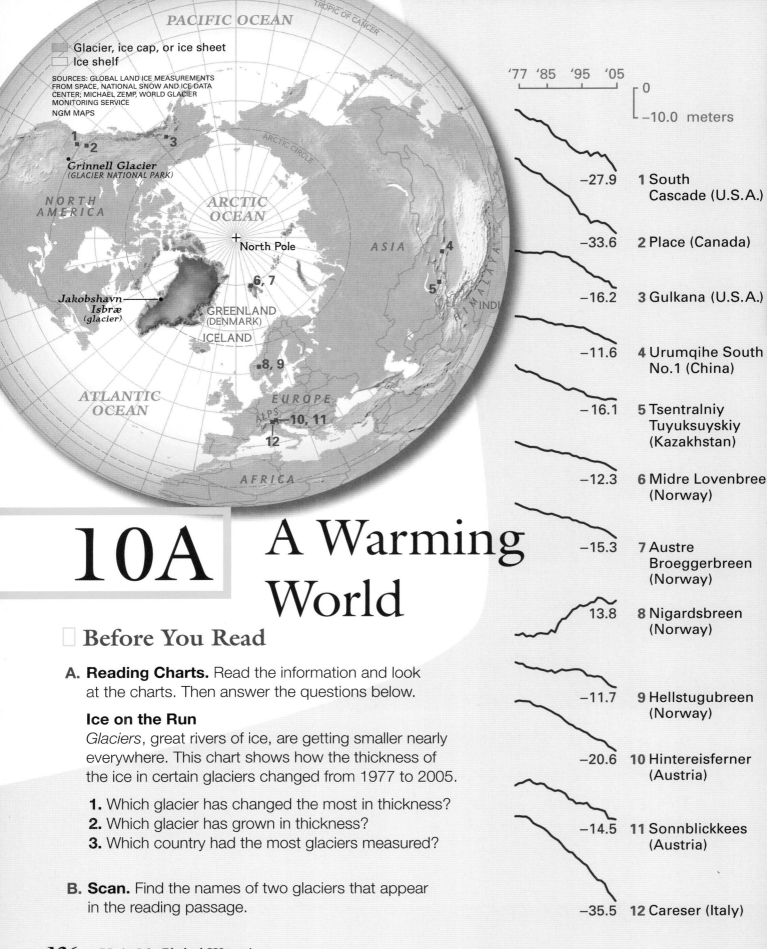

PACIFIC OCEAN

TROPIC OF CANCER

Glacier, ice cap, or ice sheet
Ice shelf

SOURCES: GLOBAL LAND ICE MEASUREMENTS
FROM SPACE, NATIONAL SNOW AND ICE DATA
CENTER; MICHAEL ZEMP, WORLD GLACIER
MONITORING SERVICE
NGM MAPS

Grinnell Glacier
(GLACIER NATIONAL PARK)

NORTH
AMERICA

ARCTIC CIRCLE

ARCTIC
OCEAN

+
North Pole

ASIA

Jakobshavn
Isbræ
(glacier)

GREENLAND
(DENMARK)

ICELAND

HIMALAYA

INDI

ATLANTIC
OCEAN

EUROPE
ALPS

AFRICA

'77 '85 '95 '05

0

−10.0 meters

−27.9   **1** South
Cascade (U.S.A.)

−33.6   **2** Place (Canada)

−16.2   **3** Gulkana (U.S.A.)

−11.6   **4** Urumqihe South
No.1 (China)

−16.1   **5** Tsentralniy
Tuyuksuyskiy
(Kazakhstan)

−12.3   **6** Midre Lovenbree
(Norway)

−15.3   **7** Austre
Broeggerbreen
(Norway)

13.8   **8** Nigardsbreen
(Norway)

−11.7   **9** Hellstugubreen
(Norway)

−20.6   **10** Hintereisferner
(Austria)

−14.5   **11** Sonnblickkees
(Austria)

−35.5   **12** Careser (Italy)

10A   A Warming World

☐ Before You Read

A. **Reading Charts.** Read the information and look
at the charts. Then answer the questions below.

Ice on the Run

Glaciers, great rivers of ice, are getting smaller nearly
everywhere. This chart shows how the thickness of
the ice in certain glaciers changed from 1977 to 2005.

1. Which glacier has changed the most in thickness?
2. Which glacier has grown in thickness?
3. Which country had the most glaciers measured?

B. **Scan.** Find the names of two glaciers that appear
in the reading passage.

The Big Thaw[1]

1   The Chacaltaya ski area in Bolivia used to be the highest in the world. Although it was less than a kilometer long, it hosted international ski competitions. Today the snow has almost gone, and so have Chacaltaya's days as a popular ski resort.

5   The ski area sits upon a small mountain glacier, which was already getting smaller when the ski area opened in 1939. In the past ten years, however, the glacier has been melting at an increased rate. As the glacier melts, dark rocks beneath it are uncovered. The sun then heats the rocks, causing faster melting. Despite attempts to make snow with snow machines, this
10   cycle seems unstoppable in the long run.

As experts debate how to solve the global warming problem, ice in mountains such as Chacaltaya and near the North and South Poles is melting faster than even the most pessimistic[2] environmentalists may have once feared. Rising air and sea temperatures are two well-known causes, but researchers
15   have recently discovered other unexpected processes that take place as glaciers melt. The effects are having an impact on humans even now, and they could change the face of the world in the future.

▲ A polar bear and her cub rest on an iceberg in the Arctic Ocean. If warming continues, the Arctic could lose its permanent ice cap by the end of this century.

[1] When ice, snow, or something else that is frozen **thaws**, it melts.

[2] Someone who is **pessimistic** thinks that bad things are going to happen.

In just six months in 2006, ▶ this glacier in Iceland lost more than 60 meters (200 feet) of ice.

▲ A white arctic fox hunts for baby seals in the ice of Norway. Scandinavia's arctic fox population, with fewer than 200 animals remaining, now faces serious threat of extinction.

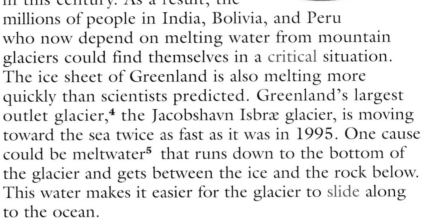

Warmer temperatures have ▶ reduced the amount of sea ice covering the Arctic.

Serious Consequences

20

The glaciers of the Himalayas and the Andes[3] could disappear in this century. As a result, the

25 millions of people in India, Bolivia, and Peru who now depend on melting water from mountain glaciers could find themselves in a critical situation. The ice sheet of Greenland is also melting more quickly than scientists predicted. Greenland's largest

30 outlet glacier,[4] the Jacobshavn Isbræ glacier, is moving toward the sea twice as fast as it was in 1995. One cause could be meltwater[5] that runs down to the bottom of the glacier and gets between the ice and the rock below. This water makes it easier for the glacier to slide along

35 to the ocean.

Many ice researchers believe that Greenland's melting, if it continues, will add at least three feet to global sea levels by the year 2100. If the ice sheet of Antarctica, now largely unaffected, begins to melt, the next few

40 centuries could see a six-foot rise in sea levels, forcing tens of millions of people out of their homes.

How can we avoid these dire[6] consequences of global warming? "We have to have a serious and immediate shift in attitude," says Laurie David, producer of the

45 prize-winning movie *An Inconvenient Truth*, which helped to raise awareness of the problem. Many believe that an attitude of hope and a desire to stay informed make a good beginning. An informed public is in a better position to help address this critical issue.

[3] The **Andes** are the largest mountains of South America.

[4] An **outlet glacier** is a glacier that moves out from the edge of an ice sheet.

[5] **Meltwater** is water released from melting snow or ice.

[6] **Dire** is used to emphasize how terrible or serious a situation or event is.

Reading Comprehension

A. Multiple Choice. Choose the correct answer for each question.

Gist

1. What was the author's purpose in writing this passage?
  a. to explain the problem of melting glaciers
  b. to suggest how to slow the melting of glaciers
  c. to illustrate how glaciers are formed and disappear
  d. to explain the causes of global warming

Vocabulary

2. In line 10, the phrase *in the long run* is closest in meaning to _____.
  a. in the near future
  b. over a long period of time.
  c. depending on the length of time.
  d. for a long time without stopping.

Detail

3. What do many researchers believe will happen by the year 2100?
  a. The ice sheet of Antarctica will begin to melt.
  b. Tens of millions of people will be forced out of their homes.
  c. The melting of Antarctic ice will add 20 feet to sea levels.
  d. Global sea levels will rise at least three feet.

Detail

4. What is happening to the ice sheet of Antarctica?
  a. It is melting dangerously quickly.
  b. Its outlet glaciers are all speeding up.
  c. Its condition isn't changing very much.
  d. It is causing a rise in global sea levels.

Did You Know?

According to a 2006 research study, nearly all of the 300 large glaciers worldwide are getting smaller.

Inference

5. Which of the following statements would Laurie David most likely agree with?
  a. Global warming is a problem that will probably fix itself over time.
  b. There is nothing the average person can do to affect global warming.
  c. Global warming is a problem, but not a very serious one.
  d. To prevent global warming, people need to change the way they think.

B. Matching. Match three of the processes with each glacier.
Put them in the correct order.

Glacier	Processes
Chacaltaya	**a.** Water gets between the glacier and the rock below.
1. ___ **2.** ___ **3.** ___	**b.** The glacier melts more quickly.
	c. The rocks absorb heat from the sun.
Jacobshavn Isbræ	**d.** Meltwater runs down to the bottom of the glacier.
4. ___ **5.** ___ **6.** ___	**e.** Dark rocks beneath the glacier are uncovered.
	f. The glacier slides more quickly.

Vocabulary Practice

A. Definitions. Read the information below. Then complete the definitions using the words in red.

In 2004, scientists were involved in a serious debate about how to solve the problem of global warming. That year, the movie *The Day After Tomorrow* gave audiences a surprising look at some of global warming's unexpected consequences. In the movie, polar ice melts very quickly, creating a variety of critical weather situations. For example, Scotland freezes, Los Angeles is destroyed by tornadoes, and New York is hit by giant ocean waves. Although the movie was successful, even environmentalists who fully believed global warming theories at the time could see that much of the science in the movie was incorrect.

1. A(n) _____ situation is very serious and dangerous.

2. If you _____ a problem, you find an answer to it.

3. _____ are people who are concerned with protecting and preserving the natural world of land, sea, air, plants, and animals.

4. When a solid substance _____, it changes to a liquid, usually because it has been heated.

5. If something is _____, it surprises you because you did not think that it was likely to happen.

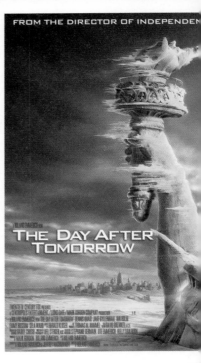

FROM THE DIRECTOR OF INDEPENDEN

THE DAY AFTER TOMORROW

B. Completion. Complete the paragraph with the correct form of the words in the box. One word is extra.

consequences	shift	slide	uncover	solve	unstoppable

Avalanches occur when a large amount of snow **1.** _____ down the side of a mountain. This moving wall of snow is nearly **2.** _____, destroying houses and buildings, and knocking down trees in its path. Some scientists warn that changes resulting from recent climate **3.** _____ may lead to a rise in the number of avalanches in certain parts of the world. Increased melting and freezing caused by climate change makes it more likely that snow will start moving. One of the more frightening **4.** _____ of avalanches is that people can be covered by a deep layer of snow, unable to escape. Avalanche rescue dogs are taught to find people under the snow, using their excellent sense of smell, and the dogs even move snow to help **5.** _____ the person.

▲ an avalanche

Word **Partnership**

Use *uncover* with:
(*n.*) uncover **evidence**, uncover **a plot**, uncover **the truth**
(*v.*) **help** uncover *something*

10B
Arctic Survivors

WALRUS HUNT
— Winter hunt route

Variable ice thickness during winter

Siorapaluk

Qeqertarsuaq

Kiatak

Start and Finish
Qaanaaq (Thule)

Inglefield Fjord

GREENLAND (Denmark)

Moriusaq

Baffin Bay

Appat

THULE AIR BASE

0 mi   25
0 km   25

SOURCE: DIGITAL GLOBE,
GOOGLE EARTH (SUMMER
SATELLITE IMAGE)
NG MAPS

North Pole
Ellesmere I.
AREA ENLARGED
GREENLAND (Denmark)
CANADA
ARCTIC CIRCLE
Maximum extent of sea ice

▲ A walrus

☐ Before You Read

A. Discussion. Look at the map above and answer the questions.
1. In which country does the hunt take place?
2. What animal is the object of the hunt?
3. In which season does the hunt take place?
4. In which city does the hunt begin and end?

B. Predict. How do the hunters travel the route shown by the red lines on the map above? Check (✓) your guess. Then read the passage to check your ideas.

❏ by small airplane   ❏ by boat   ❏ by dogsled   ❏ on skis

Last Days of the Ice Hunters

▲ Urging his dogs forward, a Greenland hunter races across sea ice that gets thinner every year.

1   Jens Danielsen kneels on his dogsled as it slides along the rough edge of a frozen sea. "*Harru, harru*," he calls out urgently. "Go left, go left. *Atsuk, atsuk.* Go right, go right." The 15 dogs in his team move carefully. Despite freezing temperatures in late March, the ice has broken up, making travel dangerous. "The sea ice used to be three feet thick

5   here," Danielsen says. "Now it's only four inches thick."

As big as a bear and with a kind, boyish face, Danielsen is a 45-year-old ice hunter from Qaanaaq, a village of about 650 people whose brightly painted houses cover a hillside overlooking a fjord.[1] He's heading toward the ice edge to find walruses, as hunters of Inuit ethnicity

10   have done for as long as memory. With his extended family and 57 dogs to feed, he'll need to kill several walruses on this trip.

▲ Hunters approach a walrus they have just killed. One walrus can feed a hunting party for four days. "Not long ago we hunted walruses from kayaks," says Danielsen, "but they killed too many of us."

Normally the ice comes to northwestern Greenland in September and stays until June. But during the past

15   few years, the ice has been thick and the hunting good for only three or four weeks. The ice shelf gives hunters access to the walruses, seals, and whales they hunt. Without it, hunting becomes nearly impossible. In one recent winter, Qaanaaq's hunters

20   found themselves without sufficient food to feed their starving dogs. The hunters asked for help, and the government responded with money while fishing corporations assisted by sending fish by airplane.

[1] A **fjord** is a narrow body of water cut into a valley by a glacier.

Today, fewer than 500 ice hunters are able to live by hunting alone. They travel by dogsled, wear skins, and hunt with harpoons.[2] At the same time, they also use guns, cell phones, and watch TV. "This changing weather is bad for us," Danielsen says, scowling.[3] "Some [of our] people have to go other ways to make a living." His wife, Ilaitsuk, who used to go with him on these hunting trips, has had to take a job at a day-care center in Qaanaaq to help pay their bills. The government now funds job training programs to help ice hunters find other employment.

▲ An ice hunter drags his dogs toward the sea ice. Sometimes the dogs sense the ice is too thin, and try to pull the hunter back.

Warmer weather does provide some opportunities. Quantities of valuable fish that prefer warmer water are increasing, and melting ice has uncovered some of Greenland's valuable natural resources—minerals, metals, and gems.[4] Electric power plants may soon be built on rivers filled by melting ice. But the last ice hunters may not be able to get used to working as fishermen, in mines, or in power plants. As Danielsen says, "Without ice, we can't live. Without ice, we're nothing at all."

[2] A **harpoon** is a long, pointed weapon with a rope attached to it, which is used to hunt large sea animals.

[3] When someone **scowls**, an angry expression appears on their face.

[4] A **gem** is a jewel or stone that is used in jewelry.

▲ An ice hunter wears a polar bear skin to teach his dogs not to be afraid of the bears. "Without knowing the polar bear's ways," says ice hunter Mamarut Kristiansen, "I would have died out here many times."

◄ Avigiaq Kristiansen, aged 15, left school to become an ice hunter. In 2004 he killed his first polar bear. "He has the will to be a great hunter," says Danielsen. But warming temperatures may mean the end of the ice hunters' lifestyle.

Reading Comprehension

A. Multiple Choice. Choose the best answer for each question.

Gist

1. What is the passage mainly about?
  a. how to hunt sea animals in Greenland
  b. how warmer weather is affecting Inuit hunters
  c. how the government is helping failed hunters
  d. how modern hunting methods are better than traditional ones

Vocabulary

2. On line 27, which phrase could best replace *at the same time*?
  a. as they do this   c. during this time
  b. on the other hand   d. quickly

Detail

3. What has made hunting with dogsleds difficult for the Inuit?
  a. Their dogs eat too much.
  b. There is too much ice.
  c. The ice is too thin.
  d. There are not enough animals.

Did You Know?

Nearly 50 percent of rising sea levels caused by global warming isn't because of melting ice. It's simply because when water gets warmer, it takes up more space.

Main Idea

4. What is the main idea of the fourth paragraph?
  a. The ice hunters have improved their hunting methods.
  b. Recently, more ice hunters have been able to improve their lives.
  c. Only the best ice hunters have been able to continue.
  d. The traditional ice hunters' way of life is disappearing.

Inference

5. Why might the ice hunters find it difficult to do other work?
  a. There is no training available.
  b. The government is unhelpful.
  c. They prefer their own traditions.
  d. There are few other jobs available.

B. Completion. Complete the information below using words from the reading passage. Write no more than two words in each blank.

1. In recent years, the winter sea ice around Greenland has been less _____ than previously.

2. The thin ice shelf makes it difficult for the hunters to get _____ to the animals they hunt.

3. Unable to hunt, the hunters must ask _____ for help.

4. In addition to money, job _____ has been provided to hunters.

5. In the future, hunters may work as _____, in mines, or in _____.

☐ Vocabulary Practice

A. Completion. Complete the information with the correct form of the words in the box. One word is extra.

access	urgent	resources	starve	sufficient	quantity

During the summer, polar bears generally eat very little. They instead rely on the large **1.** _____ of fat in their bodies built up from last year's seal hunting. At the end of a long summer without food, as they wait for the sea ice to form, polar bears are **2.** _____ and have even been known to kill and eat each other for food. Polar bears can only hunt effectively when there is sea ice. It is the sea ice that gives them **3.** _____ to their food **4.** _____, such as seals, and polar bears spend much of the year hunting on the frozen sea. Recent climate changes seem to be shortening the icy season, and there is less ice. This means the time bears have to hunt seals may no longer be **5.** _____ for their needs.

▲ A polar bear jumps across the gap in the sea ice. As the amount of ice decreases, it becomes more difficult for the bears to hunt.

B. Words in Context. Complete each sentence with the best answer.

1. A person's ethnicity is connected to his or her _____.
   a. racial or cultural background   b. level of education or wealth

2. A corporation is a _____.
   a. new technology   b. business

3. Guns are often used for _____.
   a. hunting   b. cutting

4. Something that is urgent _____.
   a. is worth a lot of money   b. must be done very soon

5. If someone funds a program, he or she _____ it.
   a. works for   b. gives money to

Usage

I'm starving!
In informal English, people often say "I'm starving!" to mean that they are extremely hungry.

Global Warming

A. Preview. Look at the diagram of the "greenhouse effect." Complete the paragraph using words from the diagram.

Without the "greenhouse effect" Earth's average temperature would be about 23°C cooler. First, sunlight travels through the **1.** _____ and warms the Earth's **2.** _____. Heat then moves up. Some escapes into space, but some is trapped by greenhouse **3.** _____ which warm the atmosphere and send heat back to the surface of the Earth.

▲ **Earth's natural greenhouse.** As the sun's rays (yellow) enter the earth's atmosphere, some are reflected back into space, or absorbed by the atmosphere. The 50% that reaches the ground is converted into heat (red). Clouds and greenhouse gases absorb most of the heat that the earth reflects back into space. Other energy includes heat caused by formation of clouds or carried by winds (blue). Normally, over time, the outgoing energy balances the incoming.

B. Summarize. Watch the video, *Global Warming*. Then complete the summary below using the correct form of words from the box. Two words are extra.

urgent	**critical**	**environmentalist**	**fund**
melt	**quantity**	**consequences**	**solve**
sufficient	**slide**	**resource**	**unstoppable**

The global warming situation has become **1.** _____. Humans are adding more and more greenhouse gases to the atmosphere. The large **2.** _____ of greenhouse gases released have been **3.** _____ to raise temperatures approximately 1°C over the past century. This is causing ice to **4.** _____ everywhere.

Different experts predict different effects including rising sea levels and floods. Other **5.** _____ such as more frequent storms and animal species dying out have also been predicted. Is the problem **6.** _____, or is there some way to **7.** _____ it? **8.** _____ tell us that we need to act **9.** _____ before it is too late. There are different ways that consumers can respond to this problem, such as saving energy, driving cars less, and reducing consumption of **10.** _____.

C. Think About It.

1. What could be some of the consequences of global warming?
2. Are you or people you know doing anything to slow down global warming?

 To learn more about global warming around the world, visit elt.heinle.com/explorer

UNIT 11

Incredible Insects

Discuss these questions with a partner.

1. Are there any insects that you particularly like or dislike? Why?

2. Which insects do you think are the most beautiful?

3. Do you think any insects are incredible? Why or why not?

▲ A Glasswing Butterfly displays its transparent wings on a fern leaf in a Costa Rican cloud forest.

147

11A Small Wonders

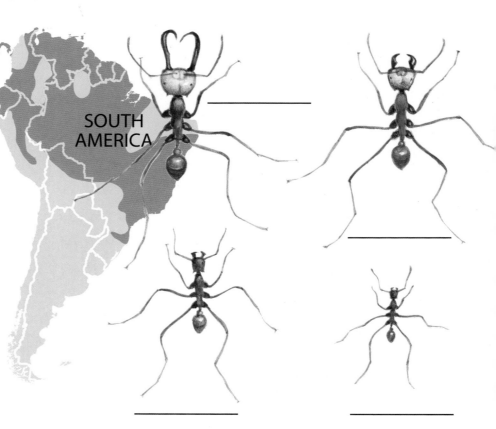

NORTH
AMERICA

Map of range of ▶
Eciton burchellii

PANAMA ─┐

SOUTH
AMERICA

☐ Before You Read

A. Labeling. The illustrations on this page show five types of ants that live in a colony of *Eciton burchellii*, found in Central and South America. Read the descriptions and label each ant with its name.

The **major** has the largest jaws. Its job is to defend the other ants.

The **queen** is the largest ant. It produces the eggs that new ants come from.

The three smallest workers kill and carry the colony's food and feed the queen and the young. From smallest to largest their names are the **minor**, the **media**, and the **submajor**.

B. Predict. Choose the best answer for the question below. Then read the passage to check your answer.

The photograph on the bottom of page 149 shows a *bivouac* of army ants. The bivouac is how the ants _____.

a. fight   **b.** eat   **c.** make a nest   **d.** climb trees

ARMY ANTS

▲ The queen of an army ant colony lives for several years. At each bivouac, the queen lays as many as 300,000 eggs.

1 Forget lions, tigers, and bears. When it comes to the art of war, army ants are among the most frightening creatures on earth.

5 With powerful mouth parts, these fighters can skillfully cut creatures much larger than themselves into pieces. Acting together in great numbers, army ant colonies[1] succeed at making tens of thousands of such kills each day. Their capabilities do have limits, though. Contrary to popular belief, they almost never take down large animals or people.

One of the best places to observe army ants is Barro Colorado, an island in a lake
10 created by the Panama Canal. The island is home to as many as 50 colonies of *Eciton burchellii*, the most studied army ant in the world. It is one of 150 types of army ants in the New World; more than 170 other types live in Asia, Africa, and Australia.

The colonies of this army ant are huge, ranging from
15 300,000 to 700,000 ants. They never stay in one place long, moving from nest site to nest site. Linking legs together, they use their own bodies to form
20 enormous nests called *bivouacs*, which they hang beneath a fallen tree. There they stay for about 20 days as the queen lays as many as 300,000 eggs.

25 When the ants go hunting, as many as 200,000 of them leave the nest in a group that broadens into a fan as wide as 14 meters. This *swarm raid* takes a slightly
30 different course each day, allowing the hunters to cover fresh ground each time.

▲ Army ants use their own bodies to form huge nests called bivouacs, which they hang beneath a fallen tree.

[1] An **ant colony** is a group of ants that live together in an organized society.

Protecting the ants wherever they go are the soldiers, recognizable by their oversized jaws. If their frightening looks don't scare enemies away, soldiers also have a powerful bite—and the attack is often suicidal.[2] Because their jaws are shaped like fishhooks, the soldiers can't pull them out again. Amazonian tribes[3] have used soldier ants to close wounds, breaking off the bodies and leaving the heads in place.

Eciton burchellii are blind and can't see what's ahead of them, but they move together in such great numbers that they easily kill the non-army ants, insects, and other small creatures that constitute their prey.[4] When the group happens upon a break in the path, ants immediately link legs together and form a living bridge so that the group can move forward without any delay.

In Japanese the word *ant* is written by linking two characters: one meaning "insect," the other meaning "loyalty." Indeed, individual ants are completely loyal to their fellow ants. They display many examples of selfless cooperation that, while certainly extreme, can't fail to win human admiration.

[2] In a **suicidal** attack, the attacker loses its life in carrying out the attack.

[3] **Amazonian tribes** are human societies living in the Amazon rainforest.

[4] An animal's **prey** are the animals it hunts and eats in order to live.

▲ The jaws of the soldier ants are shaped like fishhooks; once the soldier bites, it can't pull its jaws out again.

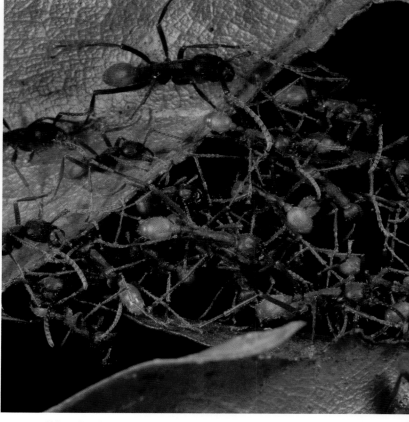

▲ When they face a gap in the path, the ants link their legs to form a living bridge.

Reading Comprehension

A. Multiple Choice. Choose the best answer for each question.

Inference

1. Why does the author tell us to forget lions, tigers, and bears?
    a. because the reading passage isn't about those animals
    b. because they are much more dangerous than ants
    c. because, in their own way, army ants can be even more frightening
    d. because there are far fewer of them than there are ants

Detail

2. Barro Colorado is _____.
    a. an island   c. a canal
    b. a lake   d. a type of ant

Detail

3. Which of the following statements about soldier ants is NOT true?
    a. They are blind.
    b. They lay many eggs.
    c. They have a powerful bite.
    d. They can be used to close wounds.

Vocabulary

4. In line 42, the phrase *happens upon* is closest in meaning to _____.
    a. meets   c. avoids
    b. causes   d. needs

Main Idea

5. What is the main idea of the final paragraph?
    a. The author is impressed with Japanese ants for their loyalty.
    b. The author is impressed with the meaning of ant in Japanese.
    c. The author is impressed with the way ants care for each other and work together.
    d. The author is impressed with how language can describe ants so well.

Did You Know?

Because army ants are blind, certain insects have learned to escape their attacks by staying perfectly still.

B. Completion. Complete the sentences with the numbers in the box. Use one of the numbers twice.

320	200,000	300,000	700,000

In 20 days a queen may lay **1.** _____ eggs.
There are over **2.** _____ types of army ants in the world.
As many as **3.** _____ ants take part in a single swarm raid.
A colony of *Eciton burchellii* contains **4.** _____ to
5. _____ ants.

Vocabulary Practice

A. Completion. Complete the information using the correct form of the words in the box. One word is extra.

| fellow | capability | constitute | loyalty | nest | observe |

Argentine ant **1.** _____ have been discovered across Italy, France, Spain, and Portugal. Taken together, they **2.** _____ a "supercolony" 6,000 kilometers long. Scientists have **3.** _____ that ants from this supercolony never fight with their **4.** _____ ants. Unfortunately, Argentine ants seem to feel no **5.** _____ toward ants from other species. They kill and eat them as they would any other prey.

▲ Argentine ants in South Africa feed on the soft tip of a shrub. They then leave the seeds without burying them, endangering the plant species.

B. Words in Context. Complete each sentence with the best answer.

1. An animal that is blind cannot _____.
a. see   b. hear

2. If you broaden a road or path, you make it _____.
a. wider   b. narrower

3. An animal's capabilities are things that it _____ do.
a. cannot   b. can

4. When insects cooperate, they _____.
a. work together   b. fight each other

5. A traffic delay could cause you to get home _____ than planned.
a. earlier   b. later

Word Link

The prefix **co-** is used to form verbs or nouns that refer to people sharing things or doing things together.

E.g. **co**operate, **co**exist, **co**-produce, **co**-worker, **co**-owner.

1.____

2.____

3.____

Unexpected Beauty

11B

☐ Before You Read

A. Discussion. Look at the photos and information below and answer the questions.

Both butterflies and moths belong to the family of insects known as *Lepidoptera*. Although they are similar, there are some differences. Most moths are active at night, whereas butterflies are active during the daytime. Moths have bodies that are hairy; the bodies of butterflies are smoother. Butterflies have bright colors on their wings, but most (but not all) moths have a dull appearance. Some butterflies can cover huge distances when they migrate: monarch butterflies, for example, travel nearly 5,000 km (up to 3,000 miles). Dragonflies belong to a different insect family, called *Odonata*. They have long, thin bodies, and strong, transparent wings.

1. Which of the photos shows **a)** a butterfly, **b)** a moth, and **c)** a dragonfly? Check your answers below.

2. How would you describe each animal pictured? Think about its colors, patterns, and shape.

B. Skim for the Main Idea. What is the reading passage mainly about? Choose **a**, **b**, or **c**.

a. How paintings of moths made an important contribution to science.
b. How moths were caught and images produced for an interesting display.
c. How scientists are photographing moths with very low populations.

1. Southern hawker dragonfly (New Mexico, U.S.A.); 2. Monarch butterfly (California, U.S.A.); 3. Tiger moth (Costa Rica)

◄ Not all moths are dull-colored: Saturn moths bring a variety of color to the rainforests of Borneo.

The Beauty of Moths

1 For many people, moths are swarming, dust-colored pests that eat our clothes and disturb us by flying around lights after dark. Not for artist Joseph Scheer. The images he creates bring out the beauty of moths, with colors, shapes, and patterns that have never
5 before been seen so clearly. "Digital[1] tools let you see things you'd never see just looking with your eyes," Scheer says. Scheer's images have been displayed around the world, and one reaction is heard everywhere: "People insist, 'No, that can't be a moth,'" says Scheer. One Swiss viewer credited the insects' lovely variety to their exotic American origin: "We don't have such nice
10 moths in our country," he declared. In fact, every country has moths that can amaze.

Moth Hunting

The process began with a moth hunt in the state of New York. Scheer would leave the lights on and the windows open overnight at his university office, then collect the moths that
15 had flown in when he returned in the morning. When the building cleaners at the university complained, he moved the hunt to his friend Mark Klingensmith's yard. "Mark's a gardener with lots of stuff growing on his property," Scheer says. "Moths like it." They set up two lights shining over a
20 plastic container on a white sheet. Then they watched, astounded,[2] as moths emerged from the darkness, flew carelessly into the sheet, and fell into the plastic container. "We got a different species every night that first season," Scheer says. "The patterns and colors were overwhelming."

▲ Scheer and Klingensmith set up a light source to attract moths for their collection.

[1] **Digital** systems record or transmit information as thousands of very small signals.

[2] If something **astounds** you, you are very surprised by it.

Scanning the Details

Using a powerful scanner[3] designed for camera film, they were able to capture detailed pictures of moths. Small moths present special challenges. "One twitch of the finger and there goes a wing," says Scheer. "I try to drink less coffee when I'm working on [them]."

▲ Joseph Scheer carefully arranges moths on a scanner. "One twitch of a finger and there goes a wing," says Scheer.

The scanner records so much information that a single moth can take 20 minutes to scan. A scan of just two small moths fills an entire CD. All that information means the size of the image can be increased 2,700 percent but still retain all the details and appear perfectly clear. You'd need a microscope[4] to see the details shown in Scheer's prints.

Scheer's work is not only a new form of art. He can also be congratulated for making a valuable contribution to the record of moths where he lives. He has helped identify more than a thousand different species. "Not from Alaska or the Amazon," Klingensmith says. "All from one backyard."

[3] A **scanner** is a machine that can take a picture of a thing for use by computers.

[4] A **microscope** is a scientific tool that allows small objects to appear larger, so that details can be seen.

▲ Over 20 species of moth cover a wall in Scheer's studio. His photographs have been shown in countries around the world.

Reading Comprehension

A. Multiple Choice. Choose the best answer for each question.

Inference

1. Why do people say, "No, that can't be a moth"?
   a. because the images are not images of moths
   b. because the moths come from foreign places
   c. because the images seem too beautiful to be moths
   d. because most countries don't have beautiful moths

Detail

2. The moth hunt moved from Sheer's office to Klingensmith's yard because _____.
   a. there were no moths at the university
   b. the cost of electricity was too high
   c. they began to catch the same types of moths
   d. the building cleaners were complaining

Detail

3. The images retain all the details even when increased 2,700 percent because _____.
   a. there is a great deal of information on the CD.
   b. the moths have very bright colors and clear patterns.
   c. very high quality paint is used to create the images.
   d. a microscope is used to prepare the images.

Vocabulary

4. In line 40, the phrase *not only* is closest in meaning to _____.
   a. more than just   c. nonetheless
   b. not at all   d. in addition

Inference

5. Why does Klingensmith mention Alaska and the Amazon?
   a. because he hopes to go to those places in the future
   b. because we would expect to see amazing moths there
   c. because moths there are very different from those in his yard
   d. because he has helped identify more than 1000 species there

Did You Know?

The largest moth in the world is the Atlas moth of Southeast Asia. It can be 30 centimeters across in length.

B. Completion. Complete the summary using **one word** from the reading to fill in each blank.

Joseph Scheer and Mark Klingensmith have created a new form of **1.** _____. They create large images that really bring out the **2.** _____ of moths. The two men collect moths which are attracted to **3.** _____ that they set up in Klingensmith's yard. They then use a **4.** _____ to record extremely detailed images of the moths. The wonderful prints are displayed around the world. In addition, the pair has done valuable work by identifying more than 1,000 **5.** _____ of moths where they live.

Vocabulary Practice

A. Completion. Complete the information with the correct form of the words from the box. One word is extra.

declare	darkness	disturb	emerge	reaction	retain

Moths and their caterpillars are a favorite food of many animals, but nature has provided them with some defenses. Some moth caterpillars feed on deadly plants. They **1.** _____ the deadly material in their bodies, which can make animals that eat them sick. When they are **2.** _____ by a bird or other enemy, the **3.** _____ of certain caterpillars is to expose large spots on their skin that look like eyes, hoping to frighten the enemy away. Most moths use **4.** _____ to protect themselves—they only **5.** _____ after the sun has gone down, making it difficult for their enemies to see them.

B. Words in Context. Complete each sentence with the best answer.

1. If someone does a job carelessly, he or she does it _____.
   a. with a lot of care   b. without being careful

2. The scientist was congratulated for making _____.
   a. a new discovery   b. a big mistake

3. An army that is overwhelmed _____.
   a. has an advantage   b. loses quickly

4. If you are credited with doing something, you are _____.
   a. believed to have done it   b. owed money for doing it

5. Someone who declares something _____.
   a. believes it strongly   b. isn't sure about it

> **Word Partnership**
>
> Use **disturb** with:
> (*v.*) **be careful not to** disturb; **do not** disturb;
> **be sorry to** disturb
> (*n.*) disturb **the neighbors**

◄ The Hawk moth caterpillar inflates part of its body as a way of defending itself from attackers.

Kenya Butterflies

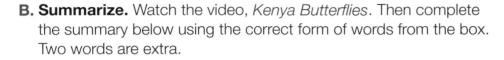
a caterpillar

A. Preview. Look at the three stages in the development of a butterfly. Which of the three stages do you think would be best to send to a customer in another country? Why?

B. Summarize. Watch the video, *Kenya Butterflies*. Then complete the summary below using the correct form of words from the box. Two words are extra.

broaden	capable	constitute	cooperate
credit	darkness	declare	delay
emerge	observe	reaction	retain

a pupa

In Kenya's Arabuko Sokoke Forest, people used to collect wild butterflies and export them to Europe and the United States. Most of the delicate insects probably died on the way. Things have improved, however, as the business has since **1.** _____ to include raising caterpillars and pupae as well. Unlike the butterfly, the pupa is **2.** _____ of living without food and in a tiny space, perfectly happy in the total **3.** _____ of a shipping box. Later, the butterflies can **4.** _____ unharmed at the customer's location.

Washington Iemba has worked hard to get local people to **5.** _____ with him in saving Arabuko Sokoke Forest. Though at first they didn't like the idea of a managed forest, he saw a change in their **6.** _____ when they saw an opportunity to make money.

a butterfly

Farmers release butterflies into their fields. The butterflies lay eggs, and the eggs become caterpillars. Farmers carefully **7.** _____ the caterpillars, waiting for the moment they become pupae. They then collect and sell most of the pupae, while making sure to **8.** _____ enough for themselves in order to grow butterflies and start the cycle again. Unlike other, slower ways of making money from the forest, the butterfly business makes money without **9.** _____, so farmers like it. "Within one month of farming butterflies one is able to generate income and use it," **10.** _____ Washington Iemba.

C. Think About It.

1. How can raising butterflies help save Abuku Sokoke Forest?
2. What do you think about the trade in butterflies? What other insects do you think could be commercially traded?

To learn more about the world of small wonders, visit elt.heinle.com/explorer

UNIT12

Going to Extremes

WARM UP

Discuss these questions with a partner.

1. Do you admire adventurous people who take risks?

Do you like to take risks yourself?

2. Where are the most extreme places a person might visit?

3. Would you like to go somewhere no one has gone before?

▲ Test pilot Major Jim Dutton flies a F/A-22 fighter plane over the Sierra Nevada mountains in California, U.S.A. The F/A-22 has over a million parts and is almost invisible to radar.

12A To the Edge of Space

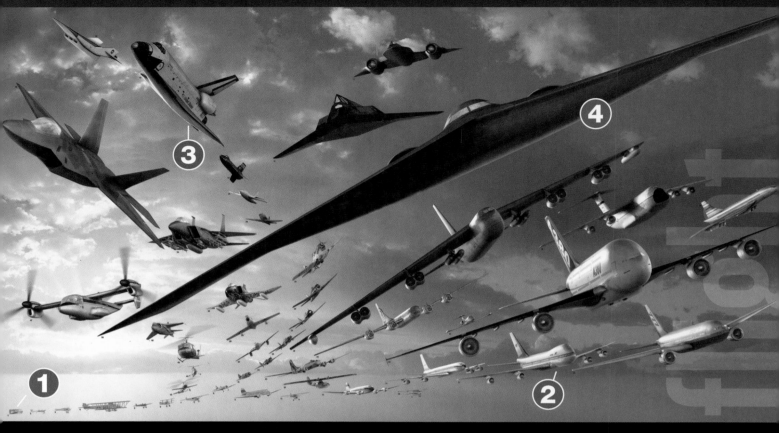

From curiosity to global industry

This illustration brings together some of the most important aircraft and spacecraft in the history of flight.

1 1903 Man's dream of flying like a bird came true with the Wright Flyer, the first powered, heavier-than-air machine to achieve controlled flight.

2 1969 Manufactured in the world's largest factory building in Seattle, U.S.A., the Boeing 747's wide-body design was able to carry more passengers than any other aircraft, reducing the cost of commercial airline travel.

3 1981 The Space Shuttle *Columbia* grabbed the world's attention when it became the first reusable spacecraft.

4 1989 The B-2 Spirit uses stealth technology to avoid radar detection as it travels long distances.

Before You Read

A. Discussion. Do you recognize any of the aircraft in the picture? What do you know about them?

B. Scan. Quickly read the reading passage to find the name of the spaceship and its designer. What is special about the spacecraft?

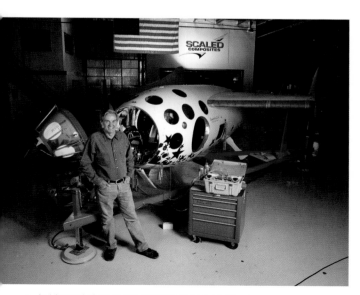

On October 4, 2004, *SpaceShipOne* dropped from its mother ship *White Knight* and flew to the edge of space—more than 100 km above the Earth's surface.

In his workshop in the Mojave Desert, California, Burt Rutan stands before the spaceship he designed.

Private Space Flight

1   Airplane designer Burt Rutan was 14 years old when the U.S.S.R. launched *Sputnik 1*.[1] He believed that government research into space travel would someday mean he too would be 5   able to journey to space. By the mid-1990s, however, Rutan had realized that waiting for the government wasn't going to work. It was then that he resolved to build his own spaceship. "If my dream was going to come 10   true—of floating[2] weightless in the black sky and being thrilled by the sight of Earth from outside our atmosphere[3]—I'd have to get things started myself," said Rutan.

The Dream of Space Flight

15   Rutan was encouraged to build his own spaceship by the history of airplane design itself. Five years after the Wright brothers'[4] first flight in 1903, the airplane was still just a dangerous curiosity. Only a dozen or so 20   people had tried flying in an airplane. Yet by 1912 hundreds of pilots had flown airplanes of different designs that were developed through private enterprise.[5] The bad designs crashed; the good designs flew. Soon factories 25   in France, England, and Germany were producing hundreds, and then thousands, of airplanes a year. "Why? I believe the answer lay in two observations: 'That's gotta be fun' and 'Maybe I can do that,'" says Rutan.

[1] **Sputnik 1** was the first man-made object sent into space to circle the Earth in 1957.

[2] Something that **floats** in or through the air hangs in it or moves slowly and gently through it.

[3] The Earth's **atmosphere** is the layer of air that surrounds it.

[4] The **Wright brothers** were two Americans who built and flew the first powered airplane.

[5] **Private enterprise** is business activity that is not directed or controlled by the government.

FEET
10 20 30 40 50 60

▲ Virgin Galactic's *SpaceShipTwo*, at 18 meters long (60 feet), will be twice as long as the original *SpaceShipOne*. It will carry six passengers and two pilots aboard.

The Dream Becomes Real

Rutan's optimism finally paid off. In 2004 his specially designed spaceship, *SpaceShipOne*, successfully entered space and made it back to earth twice in two weeks. Those were the requirements to win the ten-million-dollar Ansari X Prize, a prize designed to encourage the development of private space travel. Rutan's success got the world's attention, and various schemes to commercialize private space travel began to appear.

An Incredible Opportunity

In one such scheme, Sir Richard Branson has licensed the technology of *SpaceShipOne* for his company, Virgin Galactic, which hopes to offer people of all shapes, sizes, and ages the opportunity to visit space. Virgin's first spaceships will have two pilots and six passengers aboard. Passengers will float weightless in space for six thrilling minutes as they gaze out at space through a large window. "Of all the things we've done," Branson says, "Virgin Galactic is the one I'm most excited about. Every time I look up in the sky at night, I think about how incredible the opportunity is. People have been waiting for this moment for thousands of years."

▲ Sir Richard Branson (left) and Burt Rutan stand in front of a model of *WhiteKnightTwo*, the aircraft that will carry *SpaceShipTwo* on the first part of its flight. Named "Eve," after Sir Richard Branson's mother, *WhiteKnightTwo* can fly to over 15,000 meters (50,000 feet).

Reading Comprehension

Did You Know?

In 1919, the Orteig Prize of 25,000 dollars was offered to the first pilot to cross the Atlantic Ocean alone. Some died trying, but in 1927 Charles Lindbergh succeeded.

A. Multiple Choice. Choose the best answer for each question.

Gist

1. What is this reading mainly about?
   a. Sir Richard Branson's business
   b. famous spaceships
   c. private schemes to get into space
   d. government research into space flight

Inference

2. Burt Rutan realized he would have to build his own spaceship _____.
   a. when *Sputnik 1* was launched in the U.S.S.R.
   b. because the government space program was advancing too slowly
   c. because he was only 14 years old
   d. when he started studying the history of flight

Detail

3. What were the requirements to win the Ansari X Prize?
   a. to design a special spaceship for private space flight
   b. to encourage the development of private space travel
   c. to enter space and make it back to Earth twice in two weeks
   d. to help make ten million dollars for private space travel

Vocabulary

4. In line 36, the word *commercialize* is closest in meaning to _____.
   a. sell something to another business
   b. make money through advertising something
   c. make something well known in the business world
   d. turn something into a business

Sequence

5. Which of the following had NOT yet occurred when this article was written?
   a. *Sputnik 1* was launched.
   b. Virgin Galactic flew passengers into space.
   c. Sir Richard Branson licensed *SpaceShipOne* technology.
   d. *SpaceShipOne* won the Ansari X Prize.

B. True or False. Is the information below true (**T**), false (**F**), or not given (**NG**) in the reading passage?

1. Burt Rutan was the pilot of *SpaceShipOne*.   **T F NG**

2. Governments designed and built the first airplanes.   **T F NG**

3. Sir Richard Branson has a company called Virgin Galactic.   **T F NG**

4. Virgin Galactic's spaceships will carry eight people.   **T F NG**

Vocabulary Practice

A. Completion. Complete the information with the correct form of the words in the box. One word is extra.

scheme	launch	thrill	resolve	requirement	crash

The Ansari X Prize was **1.** _____ in 1996, but not won until 2004. Two **2.** _____ for winning the Ansari X Prize were (1) send a privately funded spaceship on two trips into space and back and (2) the spaceship had to carry added weight equal to the weight of two passengers. Twenty-six teams from seven different nations each **3.** _____ to try and win the Ansari X Prize. Several of their spaceships **4.** _____, destroying them and costing their owners a lot of money as they chased their dream of private space flight. Like the Ansari X Prize, another **5.** _____ designed to encourage people to go to space is the Google Lunar X Prize, which offers 30 million dollars to the first people to land a robot on the moon.

▲ Pilot Brian Binnie weighs in prior to flight on the SpaceShipOne.

B. Words in Context. Complete each sentence with the best answer.

1. Relatives waved to family members who were aboard _____.
 a. the ship   b. the building

2. If there is room for a dozen passengers, there must also be _____ seats.
 a. 12   b. 10

3. A license agreement with the artist is usually necessary to _____.
 a. buy a painting   b. use a song in a movie

4. It's usually a thrill to _____.
 a. open a surprise present   b. go to work

5. Something that is weightless _____.
 a. doesn't have any weight   b. hasn't been weighed

Usage

The plural form of **dozen** is dozen after a number, or after a word or expression refering to a number, such as several or a few. For example: *Please give me two dozen cookies; I've invited several dozen guests.*

Dark Descent

▲ **Top left:**
Cavers stop for a photo after making a **descent** into the New Discovery Bore Hole of Mammoth Cave, Kentucky, U.S.A.—the world's longest known cave system.

▲ **Top right:**
One of the most impressive sights in Gunung Mulu National Park, on Borneo Island, Malaysia, is the **entrance** to Deer Cave—the world's largest cave **passage**.

◄ **Bottom:**
17,000-year-old paintings of bulls and other animals crowd the cave walls at Lascaux, France. One of the bulls is 5.2 m (17 feet) long—the largest prehistoric animal painting ever discovered and one of the greatest **feats** in ancient cave art.

☐ Before You Read

A. Matching. Read the captions above. Match the correct form of each word in **bold** with a definition.

1. A(n) _____ is an impressive and difficult act or achievement.
2. A(n) _____ is a movement from a higher to a lower level.
3. A(n) _____ is a (usually long) space that connects one place with another.
4. A(n) _____ is a way into a place, such as a door or other opening.

B. Scan. Look at the reading on the next page. What name did the cavers give to the deepest point they reached?

a. Way to the Dream   **b.** Game Over   **c.** Millennium Pit

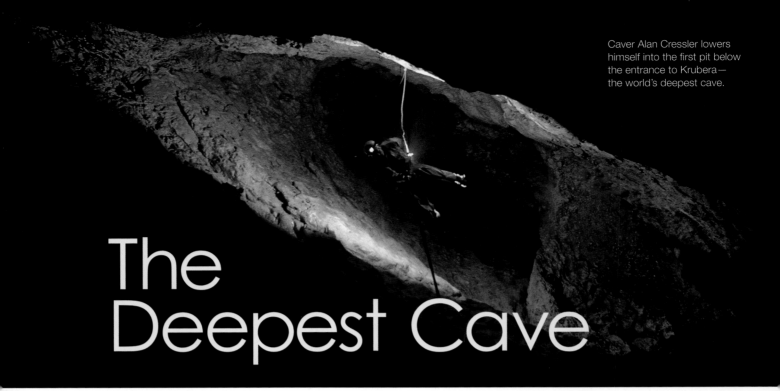

Caver Alan Cressler lowers himself into the first pit below the entrance to Krubera—the world's deepest cave.

The Deepest Cave

1   When Sergio García-Dils de la Vega kissed his girlfriend good-bye at the entrance to Krubera Cave, he promised to return the next day. But it would be two long weeks before he met her again.

García-Dils was a member of an international team exploring Krubera. The team
5   members hoped to be the first cavers to reach a depth of 2,000 meters, a feat that would be compared to conquering the North and South Poles. During the descent, team member Bernard Tourte injured himself going through a tight passage. García-Dils decided to stay with him at an underground camp, missing the chance to return to the surface before the team descended further.

10   Krubera Cave in the western Caucasus Mountains[1] is the deepest known cave in the world. Descending into Krubera, one team member said, "was like climbing an inverted[2] Mount Everest." The team members brought five tons[3] of equipment and other necessities with them, and established camps at key locations along the route. They cooked meals together, slept five and six to a tent, and worked for
15   up to 20 hours each day. They left ropes behind to ease their return ascent[4] and telephone lines to communicate with people above.

[1] The **Caucasus Mountains** lie between the Black Sea and the Caspian Sea.

[2] Something that is **inverted** is upside down.

[3] A **ton** is a unit of weight equal to 2,000 pounds or 909 kilograms.

[4] An **ascent** is an upward journey or movement.

Sergio García-Dils says good-bye to his ▶ girlfriend as teammate Bernard Tourte prepares to enter Krubera Cave.

◀ A team member crawls through a narrow passage in nearby Snow Cave.

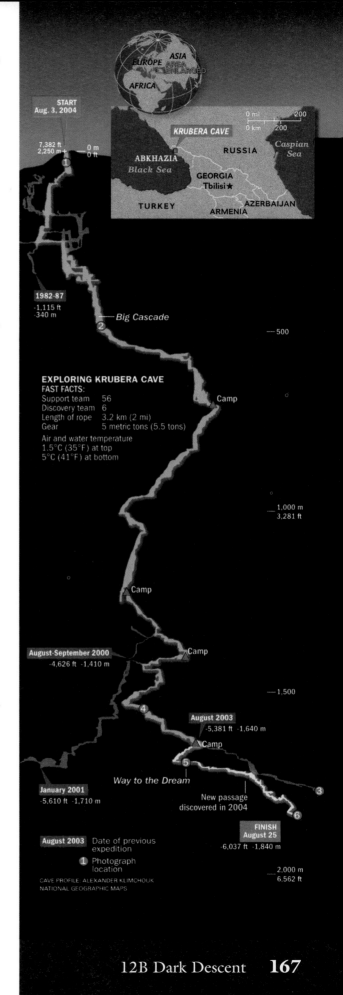

START
Aug. 3, 2004

7,382 ft
2,250 m

0 m
0 ft

EUROPE ASIA
AREA
ENLARGED
AFRICA

0 mi   200
0 km   200

KRUBERA CAVE

RUSSIA

Caspian
Sea

ABKHAZIA
Black Sea

GEORGIA
Tbilisi ★

TURKEY

AZERBAIJAN
ARMENIA

1982-87
-1,115 ft
-340 m

Big Cascade

—500

EXPLORING KRUBERA CAVE
FAST FACTS:
Support team   56
Discovery team 6
Length of rope 3.2 km (2 mi)
Gear   5 metric tons (5.5 tons)
Air and water temperature
1.5°C (35°F) at top
5°C (41°F) at bottom

Camp

1,000 m
3,281 ft

Camp

August-September 2000
-4,626 ft -1,410 m

Camp

—1,500

August 2003
-5,381 ft -1,640 m

Camp

Way to the Dream

January 2001
-5,610 ft -1,710 m

New passage
discovered in 2004

FINISH
August 25
-6,037 ft -1,840 m

August 2003   Date of previous
              expedition

① Photograph
   location

2,000 m
6,562 ft

CAVE PROFILE: ALEXANDER KLIMCHOUK
NATIONAL GEOGRAPHIC MAPS

In the third week, progress was blocked at 1,775 meters by a sump—a cave passage filled with water that gives cavers few options.
20 There are basically three techniques available: dive through it, empty it, or go around it. Gennadiy Samokhin dove to the bottom but was disappointed: "No chance to get through," he said. Searching for a way around the sump,
25 García-Dils risked entering a cascade[5] of near freezing water and discovered that his dry suit had holes in it. "The water was so cold I lost the feeling in my fingers," he said later. He, too, was unsuccessful.

30 Finally, two teammates found a way around the sump through a tight passage they called the "Way to the Dream." The team was exhilarated. The passage led to yet another sump at 1,840 meters. After a short test dive,
35 Samokhin emerged, smiling. There was a promising passage, he reported. But it would have to wait. After nearly four weeks, with supplies running low, the team had run out of time and would have to return to the surface.

40 Four weeks later, a team of nine Ukrainian cavers led by Yuri Kasjan went back to Krubera. Following the path opened by the previous team, they reached the sump at 1,840 meters relatively quickly. After much searching, a
45 pit[6] (later named the "Millennium Pit") was discovered that allowed them to pass the 2,000 meter depth. More pits and passages led them to 2,080 meters, a spot they named "Game Over." But the caving game is never over.
50 Deeper caves will probably continue to be discovered—and call out to be explored.

[5] A **cascade** is falling water.

[6] In caving, a **pit** is part of a cave that falls straight down.

Reading Comprehension

A. Multiple Choice. Choose the best answer for each question.

Gist   **1.** What is this passage mainly about?
- a. The relationship between Sergio and his girlfriend.
- b. The equipment the cavers took with them.
- c. Famous caves around the world.
- d. A journey of exploration.

Detail   **2.** Which of the following did Sergio NOT bring into the cave?
- a. his girlfriend
- b. tents
- c. ropes
- d. telephone lines

Detail   **3.** How did the cavers solve the problem of the sump at 1,775 meters?
- a. They found a way around it.
- b. They dove through it.
- c. They emptied it.
- d. They weren't able to solve it.

> **Did You Know?**
>
> Jarrod Jablonski and Casey McKinlay swam through 11.25 kilometers of water-filled underground cave in Florida. This world record dive took six hours to complete.

Reference   **4.** The word *it* on line 36 refers to
- a. the team
- b. the record
- c. the sump
- d. the passage

Inference   **5.** Why was Samokhin smiling as he emerged from a test dive?
- a. He had discovered another sump.
- b. He had possibly found a way around the sump.
- c. He knew that the team would be returning to the surface.
- d. He had found a new way to bring in supplies.

B. Matching. Match each depth with an event.

1. 0 meters _____   **a.** Game Over is discovered
2. 1,775 meters _____   **b.** The Way to the Dream begins
3. 1,840 meters _____   **c.** Gennadiy finds a way through a sump
4. 2,000 meters _____   **d.** The Millennium Pit passes this point.
5. 2,080 meters _____   **e.** Sergio left his girlfriend.

Vocabulary Practice

▲ Caver Nancy Pistole climbs out of the Well of Birds.

A. Completion. Complete the information with the correct form of the words in the box. One word is extra.

exhilarated	ease	tight	relatively	dive
necessity	option	underground	technique	rope

At the invitation of the government of Oman, expert caver Louise Hose had come to view the caves of Oman, and give the government advice on their **1.** _____ for increasing tourism at the caves. The Well of Birds is a very beautiful green pit 210 meters deep. Louise **2.** _____ her body slowly over the edge of the pit and began to lower herself down the **3.** _____. Above her, two local men stood by with guns, fascinated by a woman caver. Until recently, this area was **4.** _____ dangerous, and carrying guns was a(n) **5.** _____. The men had never seen a woman so familiar with using ropes, rappelling, climbing, and the other **6.** _____ involved in caving. When one of them fired his gun to celebrate her courage, frightened birds flew up from all around. Louise joined others in her group at the bottom, where they discovered a black pool. They **7.** _____ in and swam to the other side, where they saw the water spill out of the pool and disappear **8.** _____. They were **9.** _____ by the great natural beauty around them.

B. Definitions. Use the correct form of the words in the box in **A** to complete the definitions.

1. If you _____ something somewhere, you move it there slowly, carefully, and gently.

2. Something that is _____ is below the surface of the ground.

3. _____ are long, thing objects that can be used for tying things together or for climbing.

4. A(n) _____ is a choice between two or more things.

5. _____ are things that you must have

6. A(n) _____ is a particular method of doing an activity, usually involving practical skills.

7. If you _____ into some water, you jump in head first with your arms held straight above your head.

8. If you feel _____, you feel happy and excited.

9. A person who is _____ healthy is somewhat healthy or healthy compared to the people around him or her.

Word Partnership

Use **necessity** with:
(*adj.*) **absolute** necessity; **economic necessity**; political necessity

Young Adventurers

A. Preview. You will hear these words in the video. Use the words to label the picture.

caver	rappelling	waterfall	ledge

1. _____

2. _____

4. _____

3. _____

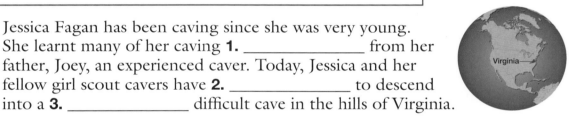

▲ Mageni Cave, Papua New Guinea, contains over five kilometers of tunnels.

B. Summarize. Watch the video, *Young Adventurers*. Then complete the summary below using the correct form of words from the box. Two words are extra.

confidence	dozen	exhilarating	relatively
rope	tight	dive	ease
option	resolve	technique	underground

Jessica Fagan has been caving since she was very young. She learnt many of her caving **1.** _____ from her father, Joey, an experienced caver. Today, Jessica and her fellow girl scout cavers have **2.** _____ to descend into a **3.** _____ difficult cave in the hills of Virginia.

To get access to the cave, the girls use **4.** _____ to gently lower themselves through the cave entrance. Once **5.** _____, the girls continue on through the passages, some of which are extremely **6.** _____. Sometimes the only **7.** _____ for the girls is to slowly **8.** _____ their way through the narrow passages on their hands and knees. It can be a frightening experience, which is why Jessica feels that **9.** _____, not strength, is the main requirement for being a caver. Eventually, the girls arrive at a huge 18-meter waterfall, an **10.** _____ sight at the end of their long journey.

Virginia →

C. Think About It.

1. What do you think are the main requirements for doing an extreme activity like caving?

2. What kinds of extreme sports and activities do you think people will do in the future?

To learn more about extreme adventures, visit elt.heinle.com/explorer

A. Crossword. Use the definitions below to complete the missing words.

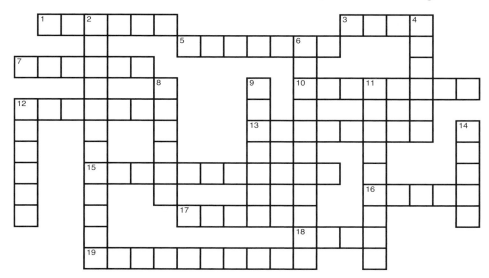

Across

1. freedom to enter or use something
3. to change from ice to water
5. to bother or trouble
7. to send into the sky or space as a rocket
10. another word for amount
12. to watch carefully
13. extremely important, or serious and dangerous
15. very happy and excited
16. to find an answer to
17. a plan to achieve something
18. a home that small animals (insects, birds) live in, or give birth in
19. enough

Down

2. the results or effects of something
4. a feeling of great excitement, pleasure, or fear
6. a quality or thing that is needed in order to be allowed to do something
8. to keep; to not lose
9. to state strongly or officially that something is true
11. something that you must have, e.g., in order to survive
12. a choice between two or more things
14. twelve

B. Notes Completion. Scan the information on pages 172–173 to complete the notes.

Field Notes

Site: Grand Canyon National Park

Location: _____, U.S.A.

Information:
- Approximately _____ people visit every year
- Shaped over _____ years by the powerful _____
- The canyon is _____ long and descends _____ at its deepest point
- Visitors can see the canyon from the 1,220-meter-high _____, or by riding the river by boat, _____, or _____
- Many of the canyon's paths were made by the _____ approximately _____ years ago
- In 1928, two _____ disappeared while riding the river — the mystery was never solved

The Grand Canyon

Site: **Grand Canyon National Park**

Location: **Arizona, U.S.A.**

Category: **Natural**

Status: **World Heritage Site since 1979**

Grand Canyon

Approximately five million people visit the Grand **Canyon** National Park every year. Some come to hike, others come to raft, but most come to simply stare at the unparalleled beauty of the park. Shaped over a period of six million years by the unstoppable power of the Colorado River, the Grand Canyon—a U.S. National Park since 1919— constitutes one of the world's most spectacular natural wonders.

The Grand Canyon is overwhelming in both its size and its history. It stretches 446 km long, with its deepest point reaching down 1,829 m. At its widest it is 29 km across. Some of the layers uncovered on the canyon's walls are 2 billion years old. It is a place where the Earth's past can be not only observed, but touched.

The majority of visitors admire the canyon from one of the many viewpoints along its edge. Others access the canyon's wonders by a more adventurous route far below—by riding the Colorado River by boat, raft, or kayak. Visitors who choose this option shouldn't expect an easy ride: "There are just two kinds of boatmen in the Grand Canyon," is an old saying. "Those who have **flipped**, and those who are going to."

▲ **Walking on Air**
Courage is a necessity for those who choose to walk the recently constructed glass pathway. Look down and you see a thrilling view of the canyon floor— 1,220 meters below your feet!

The Grand Canyon National Park is dominated by the ▲ **spectacular** canyon, carved out by the mighty Colorado River.

People of the Canyon

Native American tribes have lived in the Grand Canyon for at least 10,000 years. Many of the canyon's paths were made by the Hisatsinom people, also known as the Anasazi, approximately 1,300 years ago. The Hisatsinom also developed techniques to successfully farm in the canyon. Although they were forced to leave in the early 1900s, a small group still farms in parts of the canyon not in the National Park.

▲ The canyon's ancient rock pictures were created by native people who once lived in this remote environment.

A Canyon Mystery

Not everyone who visits the Grand Canyon comes back. Most accidental deaths are a consequence of carelessness or insufficient preparation. Occasionally, disappearances are never solved. In 1928, **honeymooners** Glen and Bessie Hyde vanished during a rafting trip on the Colorado River. Some believe they were killed when their boat crashed against the rocks, while others suspect Bessie schemed to murder her husband and then escaped. No bodies were ever found, and the mystery remains unsolved.

Glossary

canyon: a deep, steep valley formed by a river.
flip (over): to turn over, for example, into the water
honeymooners: a newly married couple taking a trip together
spectacular: extremely grand; amazing; thrilling

▲ Every year, more than 20,000 people experience the exhilaration of riding the Colorado River.

Climate

A Global View

The fastest rate of warming is occurring in the Arctic, where the ice and snow covering is getting thinner. In the mid-latitudes there are now fewer cold nights, and periods of extreme heat, known as **heat waves**, are more frequent. In 2003, during one of the warmest summers ever recorded in the Northern Hemisphere, as many as 35,000 people died in a heat wave in Europe.

Weather is the condition of the atmosphere—temperature, precipitation, humidity, wind—at a certain place at a certain time. **Climate** is the average pattern of weather for a certain region over long periods of time.

Climate affects all life on Earth: it determines what plants can grow in a region and what animals can live there. An area's climate is the result of many interacting factors, including the region's **latitude** (its distance from the Equator), **elevation** (its height above sea level), and **proximity**—or distance—to the ocean.

Climate is relatively constant, but human activity is altering climate patterns, with potentially severe consequences, such as increased flooding and **droughts** (periods of very dry weather). One observed sign of climate change is that global warming is causing Earth's glaciers to melt. If the melting continues, sea levels will rise, and low-lying coastal lands, such as Florida and Bangladesh, will be under threat.

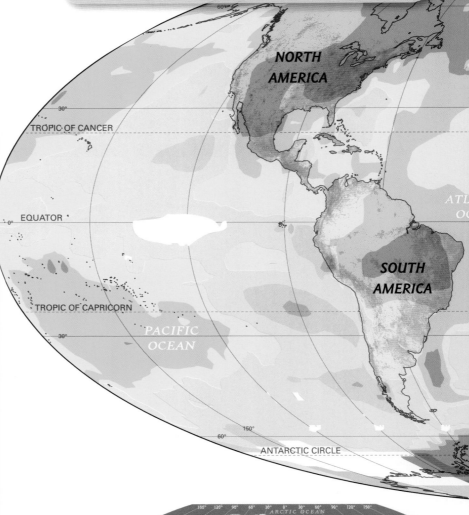

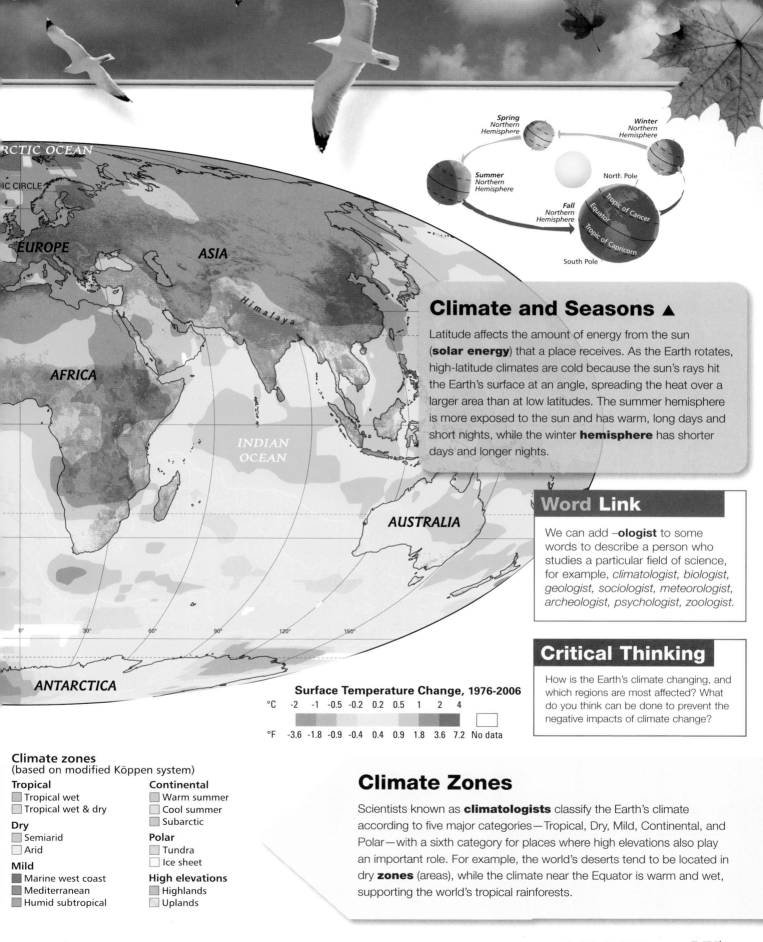

Climate and Seasons ▲

Latitude affects the amount of energy from the sun (**solar energy**) that a place receives. As the Earth rotates, high-latitude climates are cold because the sun's rays hit the Earth's surface at an angle, spreading the heat over a larger area than at low latitudes. The summer hemisphere is more exposed to the sun and has warm, long days and short nights, while the winter **hemisphere** has shorter days and longer nights.

Word Link

We can add –**ologist** to some words to describe a person who studies a particular field of science, for example, *climatologist, biologist, geologist, sociologist, meteorologist, archeologist, psychologist, zoologist.*

Critical Thinking

How is the Earth's climate changing, and which regions are most affected? What do you think can be done to prevent the negative impacts of climate change?

Surface Temperature Change, 1976-2006

°C	-2	-1	-0.5	-0.2	0.2	0.5	1	2	4	
°F	-3.6	-1.8	-0.9	-0.4	0.4	0.9	1.8	3.6	7.2	No data

Climate zones
(based on modified Köppen system)

Tropical
- Tropical wet
- Tropical wet & dry

Dry
- Semiarid
- Arid

Mild
- Marine west coast
- Mediterranean
- Humid subtropical

Continental
- Warm summer
- Cool summer
- Subarctic

Polar
- Tundra
- Ice sheet

High elevations
- Highlands
- Uplands

Climate Zones

Scientists known as **climatologists** classify the Earth's climate according to five major categories—Tropical, Dry, Mild, Continental, and Polar—with a sixth category for places where high elevations also play an important role. For example, the world's deserts tend to be located in dry **zones** (areas), while the climate near the Equator is warm and wet, supporting the world's tropical rainforests.

A. Completion. Use words in **bold** from pages 174–175 to complete the passage.

Located in the northern _____, between 40 and 60 degrees _____, most of the continent of Europe qualifies as being of the Marine West Coast climate _____. This means that the _____ there is usually mild. However, in the summer of 2003, a massive _____ hit Europe, raising temperatures to extreme levels and killing up to 20,000 people.

Many _____ believe that global warming will cause further hot summers in Europe that could be as extreme as 2003. Moreover, in places with little rainfall, rising temperatures may also cause severe _____, which can potentially lead to dangerous wildfires. In 2003, for example, wildfires raged through parts of Portugal, resulting in an estimated one billion euros (over $1.3 billion) worth of damage.

B. Word Link. We can add **–ologist** to some words to describe a type of scientist. Look at the words in the box. Which person would be most likely to do the following things (1–8)? Match the words from the box.

archeologist	**climatologist**	**geologist**	**meteorologist**
paleontologist	**psychologist**	**sociologist**	**zoologist**

1. study how animals communicate? _____
2. discover an ancient civilization? _____
3. investigate how hurricanes form? _____
4. investigate how the human mind works? _____
5. study a volcanic eruption? _____
6. make predictions about tomorrow's weather? _____
7. study the role of men and women in different cultures? _____
8. discover dinosaur bones? _____

Target Vocabulary

aboard 12A
access 10B
account (for) 1A
accurate 6B
acquire 2B
administration 8A
admire 8A
alarm 2A
analyze 3A
appeal 4B
approximate 1A
arrange 6B
aspect 1B
associate 1A
assume 1B
attach 3A
attack 1A
authority 7B
aware 2A

base 1B
beneath 3B
bite 6B
blame 5B
blind 11A
brilliant 6A
broaden 11A
budget 7B

camp 9B
capability 11A
careless 11B
categorize 6B
cave 4B
ceiling 4A
ceremony 1A
circumstance 5A
civilization 1A
claim 7A
combination 5B
commercial 7B
complex 2A

comprehend 6B
conduct 3A
confusion 6B
congratulate 11B
consent 8B
consequence 10A
conservation 6A
considerable 7A
constant 2A
constitute 11A
consume 6A
contrast 1B
contribute 8A
convenient 4A
cooperate 11A
corporation 10B
crash 12A
creature 6A
credit 11B
critical 10A
cruel 3B
cultural 4B
curious 2A
current 5A
cycle 5B

darkness 11B
debatable 3B
declare 11B
deduce 3B
delay 11A
demonstrate 9B
derive 4B
dimension 9A
display 7B
distinct 7B
distribute 5A
disturb 11B
dive 12B
domestic 2B
dominate 7A
dozen 12A

ease 12B
economic 4A
emerge 11B
emphasis 7B
employment 7A
enable 3B
enemy 2A
energize 5B
engineer 5A
environmentalist.... 10A
essence 7B
establish 4B
ethnicity 10B
evidence 1A
exclude 3A
exhilarated 12B
export 7A
expose 5A

factual 6B
feature 4A
fellow 11A
finance 8B
focus 4A
forecast 5B
freeze 3B
fund 10B

garbage 2B
gather 6B
generation 6A
government 2B
grip 9A
guard 7B
gun 10B

handle 7A
harm 2A
hero 9A
horror 6B
humid 5B
hypothesize 6B

Target Vocabulary

ignore 5A
illustrate 9A
immigration 1B
impact 9A
imply 3B
import 1B
infection 3A
initial 1A
injury 3A
interact 2A
international 9A
invade 1B

jealous 9B
jewelry 6A
journal 8A
joy 7B

labor 3B
launch 12A
layer 1B
license 12A
liquid 1A
locate 4A
loyalty 11A
luggage 2B
luxurious 3A

melt 10A
mineral 8A
misfortune 8B
modernize 4A
murder 3A

nearby 9B
necessity 12B
negative 6A
nest 11A

obedient 2B
object 4A
objective 8A
observe 11A
obtain 7B
occasionally 1B

option 12B
origin 9A
overwhelming 11B

palace 8A
partnership 2B
perceive 8A
permit 4B
plenty 2B
policy 4B
pollute 6A
predictable 8B
preserve 4B
prevent 7A
prior 8B
process 1A
professional 5B
profitable 8B
purchase 7A
pure 9A

qualify 5B
quantity 10B

reaction 11B
relatively 12B
remarkable 1B
remote 8B
renowned 7A
require 12A
reserve 9B
reside 5A
resolve 12A
resource 10B
restrict 9A
retain 11B
reunite 9B
rope 12B
rotate 5B

scheme 12A
sector 5A
selection 2B
shallow 6A

shame 9A
shift 10A
sightsee 4A
sink 5A
slide 10A
solve 10A
source 6A
starve 10B
sufficient 10B
supposedly 4B
surround 4B
symbol 9B

talent 2B
technique 12B
teenager 3A
tent 9B
theory 3A
threaten 4A
thrill 12A
tight 12B
tiny 3B
trade 7A
translator 8B

uncover 10A
underground 12B
undertake 8A
unexpected 10A
unknown 2A
unparalleled 8B
unstoppable 10A
upward 5B
urgent 10B

variety 2A
voyage 8A

wealth 3B
wedding 9B
weightless 12A
widespread 5A
wisdom 8B
wrap 9B

Olive Oil

Narrator:
Throughout much of the Mediterranean, olives are an important aspect of everyday life. Walk through any Greek market and you'll find evidence of how important they really are. Here, on the island of Naxos, you'll see them in different sizes and in different colors: green, black, brown . . .

Tourist:
"I must admit, I was around olive trees most of my life, and it wasn't until several years back that I found out the green olive and the black olive came from the same tree."

Narrator:
Like this tourist, a lot of people assume that black and green olives come from different trees. In fact, most people probably wouldn't recognize an olive tree.

This time of year, on the hills of Naxos, the olive trees have flowers on them. Without the fruit, though, the tree isn't easy to identify.

Christina Lefteris, Naxos School of Ecology:
"In this area, between Monitsia and the other village of Moni, which is up in the hills, there are some of the very old olive trees."

Narrator:
To make green olives, you need to collect them when they are still young.

Christina Lefteris:
"There are small ones and giant ones and people decide which ones they prefer. Well, I like all of them. I would never say no to any olive."

Narrator:
Not everyone has the same liking for them.

Tourist:
"I don't like them. I hate them."

Tourist:
"Yesterday, I ordered a pizza and it had olives on it and I couldn't take it."

Tourist:
"Uh, no, no. It tastes old, it tastes ugly."

Narrator:
It's true that olives are old. Some trees have been alive for thousands of years. In fact, olives have been an important part of life here since the early days of Greek civilization. In Greek tradition, Eirene, the goddess of peace, is shown carrying an olive branch. Even today, olives are associated with peace. If people want to end a war, they are said to "offer an olive branch."

Katherina Bolesch, L'Olivie Halki:
"From the olive tree, you can actually make . . . you can use everything. There is nothing you throw away."

Narrator:
Katherina Bolesch owns a remarkable shop in Naxos where everything is made from olives.

Katherina Bolesch:
"You eat the olives, you make oil from it. You can make a kind of tea from the leaves."

Narrator:
Olive oil accounts for much of Greece's olive production. To produce the best liquid, olives are collected and processed once they have become black. The sooner they are pressed, the better the oil. Used for cooking, for light, and occasionally as medicine, the oil is believed to give good health and long life to those who use it.

Christina Lefteris:
"They're very valuable for vitamins, and their oils are very healthy."

Narrator:
And the olive trees themselves also help to give the land a feeling of peace.

Christina Lefteris:
"You can have a look around and understand that all these trees are not aggressive. Their color is a little soft, all their shape is quite mild. Something that lasts long, give fruits, I think it's a good feeling of what peace means."

2 Man's Best Friend

Narrator:

Dogs are often known as man's best friend. Many societies have them as pets or rely on them to perform a variety of tasks. The story of man and dog is a complex story that goes back thousands of years and will almost certainly go on for thousands more. Dogs interact with humans in a variety of ways. Dogs such as border collies are trained to herd livestock such as sheep. Huskies pull us through some of the coldest and most dangerous places on Earth. Dogs have a sense of smell 1,000 times more powerful than our own. This means they can search for people who are lost under deep snow, or under the debris of a collapsed building, or deep in the forest. Beagles perform their duties at airports, where their sense of smell helps them to find drugs and other illegal items in people's luggage. They lead the blind and help to ease the lives of disabled people. For many, the dog is also an obedient companion—and friend.

When did this remarkable partnership start? We know now that the wolf began working with people in the distant past—roughly 14,000 years ago. Over the years, the wolf became the talented domestic pet we know as the dog. There are plenty of theories, but the real reason why humans acquired dogs is still unknown. Was it because they needed to protect each other from harm? Was it a hunting partnership? Was it a need for companionship—a type of friendship? Or was it a combination of the three? For 14,000 years the dog has played an important role in human societies. It's a partnership that's likely to continue for many years to come.

Inca Mummy

Narrator:

This girl is Quechuan, one of the native people of the Andes believed to be direct descendants of the Inca people. Clues to where she came from may lie with one of her ancient ancestors. This body of a young Inca girl was discovered in 1995 by archeologist Johan Reinhard. She was found on an Andean mountain called Ampato. Some parts of her body were mummified, preserved in ice. They named the girl after Johan, calling her "Juanita."

Johan Reinhard, Explorer:

"When we climbed the peak and found the mummy . . . then we knew we were really onto something. That they had not just worshipped it from afar, but they had actually climbed to the summit and made these sacrificial offerings."

Narrator:

Reinhard and his team walked high into the Andes, the mountain range that runs from the north of Peru to the south, dividing the country in half.

For the Inca people, these were more than just challenging places to climb—the mountains were thought to be gods. According to Reinhard, the Inca believed that if they made offerings—in this case, young girls—the mountains would treat them well. If they didn't respect the mountain gods, the people would have great problems. After their success in finding the Inca girl, Reinhard's team went back to conduct a second exploration. Their findings this time were equally important.

On the ground lay six stone circles—patterns of rock used by the Inca long ago to show the location of burial sites. After carefully digging beneath one of these circles, the body of another child was found. And not too far away, yet another body. The discovery of more bodies implies that many people were sacrificed here.

Johan Reinhard:

"This site looks like they had . . . multi-human sacrifices, not just multi-burials, and so that makes it particularly unique."

Narrator:

It wasn't easy to free the bodies or the objects that they found in the ground. The ground was frozen, and the team had to use their fingers to slowly take out the ancient pots. While the archeologists conducted their investigation, the body of the original ice maiden, Juanita, was carefully analyzed in the Peruvian town of Arequipa. She was found covered in cloth. Scientists had to separate the outer layers of clothing, which had become attached over the years.

A few months after she was discovered, Juanita was sent to Johns Hopkins University in the U.S., where a team of scientists looked for clues about her death. They used modern technology to deduce that a powerful blow to the side of her head had broken her skull. According to their theory, it was this injury that ended the young girl's life.

Like all mummified bodies found in the Andes, Juanita enables us to understand more about the ancient Inca people who once lived in these mountains.

Juanita could be evidence of a connection with the people, like this little Quechuan girl, who live here now.

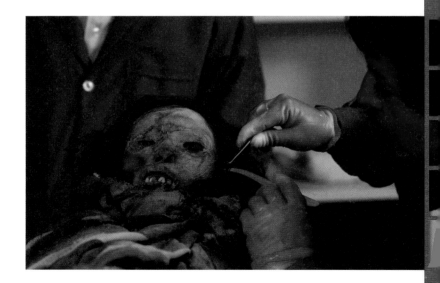

4 Mountain Train

Narrator:

There are many trains in India, but none may be as special as the Darjeeling Himalayan Railway. It's so small that people call it the "toy train." It also may be the slowest train in the world.

Every day, a six-man team prepares the old engine with water, coal, and steam before permitting it to make the long mountain climb. People here have depended on the railway since it was established in 1881. A familiar feature for locals, the train has become almost like an old friend.

Passenger:

"But as long as it is there, yes, it is a part of life."

Narrator:

Every day, the toy train climbs over 2,250 meters. Tight mountain turns become increasingly difficult as the train climbs toward Darjeeling, a town located at the foot of the Himalayas and surrounded by some of the tallest peaks in the world.

The winding route means the train needs to use narrow tracks and travel at a very slow speed. Although the entire trip is about 80 kilometers, on a slow day it can take up to ten hours! Despite the inconvenience, the train appeals to both locals and sightseers. Nobody seems to object to the train's slow speed—in fact, most seem to derive a lot of pleasure from it. While other historic trains may be threatened by modernization, the Darjeeling Railway has been carefully preserved for its cultural importance.

For fans of this train, being slow is actually a good thing. As the sign says, "slow" has four letters, so has life. "Speed" has five letters, so has death.

Birth of a Hurricane

Narrator:

At 6:10 a.m. on Monday, August 29th, a Category 4 hurricane named Katrina reached the Louisiana coast, destroying almost everything in its path. What were the circumstances that led to this catastrophic storm?

Five days earlier, on August 24th, the temperature off the coast of the Bahamas was almost 30 degrees Celsius. Humid air was rising upward from the warm waters of the ocean. As the warm, wet air rose, it condensed and formed a system of thunderstorms. This condensation releases heat, which warms the cool air of the atmosphere, causing it to rise. As that air rises, more warm air from the ocean takes its place. This creates a cycle which continuously moves heat from the ocean to the atmosphere. The movement creates a pattern of wind that begins to move around and forms a center. Occasionally, one such rotating wheel of thunderstorms gathers strength, feeding on the combination of moisture and heat. When the winds of Tropical Depression 12 reached almost 63 kilometers an hour, Tropical Storm Katrina was born.

Most extreme tropical storms happen in the open sea, where they do little harm. Some, like Katrina, arrive on the land. Katrina moved slowly—sometimes as slow as nine kilometers per hour—but she was getting stronger and heading toward Florida.

Katrina only qualified as a Category 1 hurricane when she touched the Florida coast and moved out into the Gulf of Mexico. In the Gulf, the water reached a very warm 30 degrees Centigrade. These warmer waters caused Katrina to become stronger and more energized.

After three days moving over the warm waters of the Gulf, Katrina grew to a Category 5 hurricane, with winds of more than 250 kilometers an hour. Before arriving on land, Katrina was a Category 4 hurricane, but that was still extremely strong. With powerful winds and a giant wave, or storm surge, over six meters high, Katrina was still the most destructive storm to hit the area in 36 years. The danger could no longer be ignored. Once over land, the states of Louisiana and Mississippi became exposed to Katrina's destructive winds. At the same time, now that it was away from the warm waters of the Gulf, the storm began to weaken. Twelve hours after reaching land, Katrina was no longer a hurricane, with top winds of just over 100 kilometers an hour.

6 Swimming with Sharks

Narrator:

Many people like to go diving when they are on vacation. This family are getting ready to dive off the coast of Florida. But this is no ordinary dive. It may be difficult to comprehend, but there are some people who will pay a lot of money for the opportunity to dive . . . with sharks. Shark tourism is big business in some places, and that's raising questions about how close people should get to them.

Kathy Sonnemann, Diver:

"I actually had a chance to lay down on the bottom, and the sharks were right in front of me. And I could see their mouths and their eyes and they actually brushed up against me. And it was just really cool."

Narrator:

Several times a week, diving instructor Jeff Torode takes customers to swim and even play with these harmless nurse sharks. But he no longer feeds the sharks as he once did. In January 2002, Florida became the first U.S. state to ban the feeding of marine wildlife. That followed a summer of shark attacks which caused a lot of negative publicity. The horror of shark attacks makes many people react against them. Some tourists, though, believe they should be able to get close to sharks, including dangerous varieties. Divers in the waters of the Florida Keys, for example, often interact with bull, reef, and lemon sharks—all of which have occasionally attacked people.

But despite such attacks, it would be inaccurate to say that sharks kill a lot of people. In fact, dogs bite more people than sharks do—and you have a greater chance of getting killed by lightning, bees, or snakes than by a shark. In one recent year, there were just 60 shark attacks against humans and just three deaths worldwide. Still, some people think that it's foolish to feed sharks and bring them close to busy beaches.

Bob Dimond has been a diver for 30 years. He's still diving today—although he's worried that sharks may be losing their fear of humans.

Bob Dimond, Marine Safety Group:

"Feeding sharks. The reason—or the purpose—that people feed sharks is to attract them to human beings. That's why they do it. You may not be a shark's prey, but when sharks learn to associate humans with food, they approach you, investigating to see if you have food."

Narrator:

For Dimond, that's reason enough for banning the feeding of sharks. Bob has created the Marine Safety Group. Their goal is to ban all shark feeding.

Bob Dimond:

"If you feed a wild animal, you are greatly increasing the chance that that animal will attack humans. That is why it is banned in every national park in the United States and Canada."

Narrator:

Shark feeding has never been directly associated with an attack on a human. When a shark does strike, it is usually "hit and run." It bites and then quickly releases the person and disappears. Researchers hypothesize that these sharks may have confused a human with a seal or another animal that they would normally kill.

For divers such as this 14-year-old girl, the opportunity to go diving with sharks is a chance to understand them better. Meeting them up close, she says, has made them a little less terrifying.

Trista Sonnemann, Diver:

"I thought they'd be more scary, but they're not. They were a lot more calmer than I thought they would be.

I thought it was pretty cool. It was really cool. A once-in-a-lifetime experience."

Madagascar Perfume

Narrator:

The island of Madagascar is renowned for its distinctive wildlife. But these Swiss scientists are interested more in the island's smells and tastes—and the chance to find essences for entirely new perfumes and flavors . . .

This scientist says he discovered a flower yesterday. The bud has just opened, and he expects the flower's scent to be very appealing, perhaps primarily a mix of vanilla and jasmine. The Swiss team goes by river, deep into the forest, then by balloon up into the treetops, hoping to obtain new flowers and fruits. The scientists bring the essences back to the laboratory, where they use technology to recreate the scents.

Professor Roman Kaiser, Chemist:

"I'm quite happy it's already very close to this beautiful stephanotis scent as I experienced it on the Tampolo River."

Narrator:

The scents and flavors will be used in a variety of products for purchase in stores all over the world—everything from bath products to fruit juices. This scientist says they have found two or three types of fruit whose taste is still unknown. They may be able to use these new essences to change existing flavors, and perhaps derive entirely new flavors.

But not all the discoveries are special.

Willi Grab, Chemist:

"Juicy? Acidic? A little bit earthy? Watery? Nothing fantastic. Nothing special!"

Narrator:

Only a few of these scents and flavors will be exported to markets and eventually displayed in stores. But the next time you're purchasing perfume, you could be smelling "the secrets of Madagascar."

8 Crossing Antarctica

Narrator:

They were two women with one goal. Liv Arnesen and Ann Bancroft dreamed of becoming the first women in history to ski across Antarctica. And on February 11, 2001, they achieved their goal. The crossing had been completed only once before, by a team of two male explorers. The story of Liv and Ann's unparalleled adventure became the basis for a book, in which they shared their reasons for exploring the planet.

Ann Bancroft, Explorer:

"People ask us, what is there left to explore? There's certainly you to explore, you know, internally, and the trips draw out new things in you as an individual. You never know how you're going to be in your moment of truth."

Narrator:

Prior to leaving for Antarctica, the two women undertook a demanding training schedule. They practiced skiing down roads, pulling tires behind them. The hardships got worse when they arrived in Antarctica. There were very strong, sometimes unpredictable winds of up to 160 kilometers an hour. And, of course, it was extremely cold. Sometimes they had to use their food to warm their fingers, to get the blood moving again. During their adventure, Liv and Ann shared their story with people from 150 countries through an online journal.

Ann Bancroft:

"I think the thing that's fabulous about opening the story up to others is it comes back. And it's not just remarking on what we're doing. What we ended up getting were other people's dreams."

Narrator:

The Internet site enabled the two women not only to share their own adventures but also to relate to other people's experiences in different parts of the world.

Liv Arnesen, Explorer:

"What do you think of this, eh, Ann? A little bit scary?"

Ann Bancroft:

"We all understand overcoming struggles, for instance, finding support—you know, you never do anything alone, those kinds of themes."

Narrator:

Despite their remote location, the women still felt connected with people around the planet. Liv and Ann are now planning their next adventures. Their next goal is to travel to the other end of the world—and to become the first women in history to cross the Arctic Ocean.

Nubian Wedding

Narrator:

It is modern, yet has its origin in the past. The Nubian wedding ritual, celebrated by the entire village for seven days and nights. The air is perfumed by incense and filled with the sound of drums and joyful Nubian songs.

Two years ago, Sheriff's family told him it was time to get married. So he visited every home in the village, looking for the right girl. Then he saw Abeer, and he ran home to tell his mother he had found his bride. The two young people were not reunited until just before their Muslim wedding.

Sheriff, Groom:

"The first time I saw her, when the Sheik came to sign the book, I looked at her picture to make sure it was her."

Narrator:

After the legal papers are signed, seven days of celebration begin. Each day, early in the morning, the party begins to fill the nearby streets. The bride is painted all over with henna. One day before the wedding ceremony, the groom's bed is taken outside to be bathed in sweet-smelling incense. The groom himself is also perfumed. The scents, which will last for weeks, are supposed to get his blood moving and give him strength.

Who are the Nubians and where did they come from? They traditionally lived along the banks of the Nile River, in what is now southern Egypt and northern Sudan. But in the 1960s, that changed. In Egypt, the Nubian population was removed by the Egyptian government, and their ancient lands were flooded when the Aswan dam was built.

Mohammed Nour came here at the age of 12. His family left their simple home made of mud and moved into a government house.

Mohammed Nour:

"Even though there, in the old village, there was no electricity or means of transportation like we have here now, still life there was better. There we used to keep our Nubian traditions and Nubian language. Nubian language could be endangered here today."

Narrator:

On the final night of the wedding, the village is served a celebratory meal of meat and rice in front of the groom's house. Then, gripping a sword and whip in his hands, the groom leaves his parents' home and leads his neighbors through the streets, singing religious songs. Some time after midnight, the groom picks up the bride, and they arrive at the party. They spend all night dancing and singing, from early evening until noon the next day.

The word *Nubia* derives from an ancient word for gold and refers to the gold mines for which the area was once famous. That gold still shines today as a friend wraps the bride in decorative jewelry.

It's now past 3:00 in the morning, but the party has just begun. After the exchange of rings, the groom's mother kisses her son and his new bride as they begin their life together, carrying on their ancient customs—Egyptian by nationality, but Nubian by tradition.

10 | Global Warming

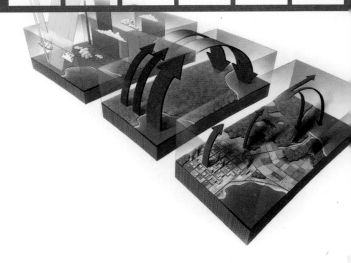

Narrator:

For 2.5 million years, the Earth's climate has varied, moving between extremely cold ice ages and warmer periods. But in the last century, Earth's temperature has risen unusually fast—by nearly one degree Celsius. Scientists believe that human activity is making the temperature go up, a process known as global warming. And many are worried the situation is becoming critical.

Ever since the Industrial Revolution, factories, power plants, and, more recently, cars have burned fossil fuels such as oil and coal, releasing huge quantities of carbon dioxide and other gases into the atmosphere. These greenhouse gases trap heat near the Earth through a naturally occurring process called the "greenhouse effect." The greenhouse effect begins with the sun and the energy it sends to the Earth. The Earth and the atmosphere take in some of this energy, while the rest goes back into space. Naturally occurring gases in the atmosphere trap some of this energy and reflect it back, warming the Earth. Scientists now believe that the greenhouse effect is being strengthened by greenhouse gases that are released by human activity.

Evidence for global warming includes a number of unexpectedly warm years in recent years. Scientists report that 1998 was the warmest year in measured history and 2005 was the second. Studies of ice cores show that greenhouse gases have reached their highest levels in the past 420,000 years. Arctic sea ice is also shrinking. According to NASA studies, the area covered by Arctic sea ice has decreased by about ten percent in the last 30 years. If countries continue to use a lot of fossil fuel resources, the amount of greenhouse gases in the atmosphere will continue to rise. Researchers predict that temperatures will increase by about one to six degrees Celsius by the end of the century.

So what are the possible consequences for the environment of these rising temperatures? Some climate models say there will be only slight changes. Others predict rises in sea levels that could flood coastal areas. Changing weather patterns could make huge storms like hurricanes more frequent. Extreme droughts could become more common in warm areas, and some animals, which may not be able to adapt, could face extinction.

There is still a lot to be learned about global warming. However, many believe that governments and corporations can help to reduce the impact of global warming by cutting greenhouse gas emissions. Consumers can also help by saving energy around the house, for example, by using light bulbs that require less energy and driving fewer miles each week. These simple changes may help to keep the Earth cooler in the future.

Kenya Butterflies

Narrator:
The Abuku Sokoke Forest is home to more than a third of Kenya's 870 species of butterfly. The demand for unusual butterfly species for public and private collections has long been a threat to natural environments such as this Kenyan forest.

In the past, butterfly collectors caught thousands of insects from the wild, sending live animals to Europe and the U.S. It's sad to say that most probably died before they arrived. Several years ago local farmers decided to use their capabilities for a different project—rearing caterpillars. The caterpillars are sent around the world as pupae and arrive just in time to become adult African butterflies. These butterflies have a survival rate of nearly 100 percent.

Wellington Combo, Kenyan Wildlife Service:
"Abuku Sokoke Forest is important because it is the largest remaining coastal forest in East Africa."

Narrator:
The main threats to the forests, he says, are cutting down the trees to make places to live. Now people are better educated, and they can see the benefits of keeping the forests. They are getting income from butterfly farming, beekeeping, and from plants that can be used for medicine.

Wellington Combo:
"So at least they have seen the benefits of having the forest stay."

Narrator:
This is the project's headquarters, right in the heart of the forest. Farmers from all over the region come here to breed the butterflies. The price of each species varies a lot according to international supply and demand, so these farmers have to know which butterflies buyers want to buy.

Much of the credit for the project's success must go to this man—Washington Iemba.

Washington Iemba, Kipepeo Butterfly Project:
"The Butterfly Farm started in 1993, and the objective then was to develop local support for the conservation of Abuku Sokoke Forest."

Narrator:
Until recently, he says, many of his fellow community members objected to the way the forest was managed because they couldn't derive income from it. But he says that farming butterflies has now become attractive, as it constitutes a new source of income.

Washington Iemba:
"Now most of the farmers even know the botanical names like any university student."

Narrator:
The process involves community members first catching a small number of butterflies. These are then carefully released into a closed area. The females lay their eggs, and caterpillars finally emerge. After they pupate, or enter their cocoons, the caterpillars are brought to the project center, where the farmers receive money for their work.

Washington Iemba:
"What do you have for us today? These ones are very good. In fact, you can see they are shaking, shaking, showing that they are still very fresh, but if you remember to have Monideas, because Monideas at the moment is the one that has a lot of market space."

Narrator:
Each farmer retains a small number of pupae so that the entire process can be repeated without having to collect new insects from the wild.

Washington Iemba:
"In a year, we sell pupae worth almost 60,000 U.S. dollars. Of these, 60 percent goes to the local communities, mostly for food, and school uniforms, school fees, hospital bills. The most attractive aspect has been that, unlike other programs used in forest areas, this has quick returns. Within one month of farming butterflies, one is able to generate income and use it, and therefore adding more value to the program itself."

Narrator:
In the beginning, 100 workers cooperated to start the project. Now there are more than 1,000. The success of the Butterfly Project has resulted in similar projects being established in parks all over Kenya.

12 | Young Adventurers

Narrator:
These Girl Scouts from Virginia are on an outing. But this is no ordinary camping trip. These girls are going caving. Jessica Fagan is 17 and has been caving since she was a little girl. Her father, Joey, is an experienced caver and the leader of this trip. It was Jessica's love for the sport that led to today's adventure. She says the challenge of getting through a difficult cave together creates a special bond.

Jessica Fagan, Girl Scouts of Virginia:
"To do something challenging and talk about, I guess, our lives. It's very special, I guess, how much you bond with people. There are girls that I've caved with years and years ago that I still keep in touch with."

Narrator:
Somewhere in these hills in the heart of Virginia lies the entrance to their destination. But it's not easy to enter. Using ropes to rappel into the cave is the only real option for going underground.

Inside, it's very dark, cold, and damp. Lights and warm clothes are both necessities for the cavers. After only a few feet, they're at a very tight spot called "the chimney." It's a drop of nine meters.

Guide:
"You can use this as a hand hold, so you can lower yourself."

Narrator:
Sometimes the only technique you can use in narrow sections of the cave is to carefully slide and squeeze, and slowly ease your way through. It's a lesson in confidence, a lesson that Jessica learned early on when she had to go on her hands and knees over a ledge. Although the potential fall was only just over a meter, it was still a frightening experience. But, she says, in the cave, everyone encourages each other, and no one gets too scared. Jessica explains that the main requirement is confidence, not strength.

Jessica Fagan:
"A lot of the caving challenges are not about how tall or how strong or how big you are, but about how confident you are. You need to be optimistic and be like, I can do it, I can crawl through this, I can climb up that, even though you had this thing in the back of your mind saying that you couldn't and you did. Then you learn something about yourself and you grow as a person."

Narrator:
After descending more than 60 meters below the surface, they arrive at a special part of the cave—an underground room over 300 meters long and over 20 meters high.

Guide:
"This is actually one of the largest rooms in the state of Virginia."

Narrator:
It's a room as large as three football fields, created out of the surrounding rock by drops of water over millions of years.

Jessica Fagan:
"It's taken millions and millions of years to form the caves, and sometimes when people go caving, I don't think they realize how special that is, and how important it is to conserve them, and how important it is to not take things off or to write their names."

Narrator:
Just by listening, the group can tell they're getting closer to something else very special—a huge 18-meter waterfall, a thrilling and exhilarating sight at the end of their long journey.

Jessica Fagan:
"There's so much more to us and to this world than humans. Nature is bigger than we are, and it will be here, the caves will be here, even if we aren't."

oto Credits

mes Balog/National Geographic Image Collection 4 (t, l) Flip Nicklin/
ational Geographic Image Collection, (c) John Burcham/National
Geographic Image Collection, (b) Joel Sartore/National Geographic Image
Collection, 5 (t, l) O. Louis Mazzatenta/National Geographic Image
Collection, (t, r) Robb Kendrick/National Geographic Image Collection,
(b, l) Mike Parry/Minden Pictures/National Geographic Image Collection,
(b, r) David Doubilet/National Geographic Image Collection, 6 (t, l)
Abraham Nowitz/National Geographic Image Collection, (t, r) Ira Block/
National Geographic Image Collection, (c, l) NGM Art/National
Geographic Image Collection, (b, l) Nick Norman/National Geographic
Image Collection, (b, c) James Balog/National Geographic Image
Collection, (b, r) Flip Nicklin/Minden Pictures/National Geographic Image
Collection, (c, r) Stephen Alvarez/National Geographic Image Collection,
7 (t, l) Tim Laman/National Geographic Image Collection, (b, l) Tim
Laman/National Geographic Image Collection, (b, c) Bobby Model,
National Geographic Image Collection, (b, r) Sisse Brimberg/National
Geographic Image Collection, (c, r) Eric Isselée/Shutterstock, (t, r) Alex
Staroseltsev/Shutterstock, 9 Fritz Hoffmann/National Geographic Image
Collection, 11 (t) Ira Block/National Geographic Image Collection,
12 (all) Ira Block/National Geographic Image Collection, 14 Stephen Van
Horn/Shutterstock, 15 (c) Juanmonino/iStockPhoto, (b) Pawel Strykowski/
Shutterstock, (b, r) Rohit Seth/Shutterstock, (t) Funwithfood/iStockPhoto,
(c, r) David Hsu/Shutterstock, 16 Ira Block/National Geographic Image
Collection, 17 (t) cloki/Shutterstock, (r) Alex Staroseltsev/Shutterstock,
(c, r) Eric Gevaert/Shutterstock, (c, l) Stefan Petru Andronache/
Shutterstock, (l) Robyn Mackenzie/Shutterstock, (b, l) Marc Dietrich/
Shutterstock, (b, r) Jason Lugo/iStockPhoto, 19 (r) Jump Photography/
Shutterstock, 20, 179 (t) Maceofoto/Shutterstock, 21 Karine Aigner/
National Geographic Image Collection, 22 (t, l; b) Flip Nicklin/National
Geographic Image Collection, (t, r) Mike Parry/Minden Pictures/National
Geographic Image Collection, 23 Flip Nicklin/National Geographic Image
Collection, 24 (t) Flip Nicklin/National Geographic Image Collection,
26 (t) Tui de Roy/Minden Pictures/National Geographic Image Collection,
(b) Gulf of Maine Cod Project, NOAA National Marine Sanctuaries;
Courtesy of National Archives, 27 Robert Clark/National Geographic
Image Collection, 28 (t) Alaska Stock Images/National Geographic Image
Collection, (b) Richard Olsenius/National Geographic Image Collection,
29 (t, b) Richard Olsenius/National Geographic Image Collection,
31 (t) U. S. Customs and Border Protection, (b) Yuri Arcurs/Shutterstock,
32 (t, l) Maxim Kulko/Shutterstock, 32, 180 (b, c; t, r) Eric Isselée/
Shutterstock, 33 Kenneth Garrett/National Geographic Image Collection,
34 (t) DAMNFX/National Geographic Image Collection, (b) Getty Images,
(c) Kenneth Garrett/National Geographic Image Collection, 35 (t) Kenneth
Garrett/National Geographic Image Collection, (b) DAMNFX/National
Geographic Image Collection, 36 (t) Kenneth Garrett/National Geographic
Image Collection, (c, l) NGM Art/National Geographic Image Collection,
38 (t) O. Louis Mazzatenta/National Geographic Image Collection,
(c) Seoul National University, 39 (all) Kenneth Garrett/National
Geographic Image Collection, 40 (b) Kenneth Garrett/National Geographic
Image Collection, 41 (all) Kenneth Garrett/National Geographic Image
Collection, 44, 181 (t) Stephen Alvarez/National Geographic Image
Collection, 46–47 (bg) O. Louis Mazzatenta/National Geographic Image
Collection, 47 (b) Cheryl Nuss/National Geographic Image Collection,
48–49 (t from l) btrenkel/iStockPhoto, Valentin Casarsa/iStockPhoto,
Angel Herrero de Frutos/iStockPhoto, Vikram Raghuvanshi/iStockPhoto,
49, 50 (t, r) Sarah Leen/National Geographic Image Collection,
51 Steve McCurry/National Geographic Image Collection, 53 (t, b)
Ira Block/National Geographic Image Collection, 54 (all) Ira Block/
National Geographic Image Collection, 56 (t) Donald R. Swartz/
Shutterstock, (b) Paul Chesley/National Geographic Image Collection,
57 (t, l) Mattias Klum/National Geographic Image Collection, (c, l)
Abraham Nowitz/National Geographic Image Collection, (r) Justin
Guariglia/National Geographic Image Collection, 58 (t) Abraham Nowitz/
National Geographic Image Collection, (b) William Albert Allard/National
Geographic Image Collection, 59 (c, b) Abraham Nowitz/National
Geographic Image Collection, 61 Entertainment Press/Shutterstock,

62, 182 (t) Steve McCurry/National Geographic Image Collection,
63 Todd Gipstein/National Geographic Image Collection, 64 Jocelyn
Augustino/FEMA, 65 (t) Tyrone Turner/National Geographic Image
Collection, 66 (t, r) David Burnett/National Geographic Image Collection,
(c, l) Tyrone Turner/National Geographic Image Collection, 68 (t, r)
Christa DeRidder/Shutterstock, 69 (t) NASA, 70 (t) Annie Griffiths Belt/
National Geographic Image Collection, (b) Harold F. Pierce/NASA/
National Geographic Image Collection, 71 David Burnett/National
Geographic Image Collection, 73 Clint Spencer/iStockPhoto, 74, 183 (t)
Tyrone Turner/National Geographic Image Collection, 75 David Doubilet/
National Geographic Image Collection, 77 (all) Chris Newbert/Minden
Pictures/National Geographic Image Collection, 78 (l) Norbert Wu/Minden
Pictures/National Geographic Image Collection, (r) Tim Laman/National
Geographic Image Collection, 80 Norbert Wu/Minden Pictures/National
Geographic Image Collection, 81 David Doubilet/National Geographic
Image Collection, 82 (all) David Doubilet/National Geographic Image
Collection, 83 (t) David Doubilet/National Geographic Image Collection,
(c) Mike Parry/Minden Pictures/National Geographic Image Collection,
84 Norbert Wu/Minden Pictures/National Geographic Image Collection,
85 Universal/The Kobal Collection, 86, 184 (t) Brian J. Skerry/National
Geographic Image Collection, 87–89 (all except globe) David Doubilet/
National Geographic Image Collection, 90 (t, b) 1001nights/iStockPhoto,
(c) Serdar Yagci/iStockPhoto, 91 (t, l) Tammy Peluso/iStockPhoto, (t, c)
Andrew Simpson/iStockPhoto, (t, r) Le Do/iStockPhoto, 92 Tammy Peluso/.
iStockPhoto, 93 Mattias Klum/National Geographic Image Collection,
94 (c, r) Ihor/Shutterstock, (t) Jonathan Blair/National Geographic Image
Collection, (b) Kip Ross/National Geographic Image Collection, 95 (t)
Panoramic Stock Images/National Geographic Image Collection, (c) Sisse
Brimberg/National Geographic Image Collection, 96 (t) Sisse Brimberg/
National Geographic Image Collection, (b, l) Taylor S. Kennedy/National
Geographic Image Collection, (b, r) Joel Sartore/National Geographic
Image Collection, 98 Pablo Corral Vega/National Geographic Image
Collection, 99 (b) Robb Kendrick/National Geographic Image Collection,
(bg) Markus Guhl/iStockPhoto, 100 (t) Robb Kendrick/National
Geographic Image Collection, (b) Joel Sartore/National Geographic Image
Collection, 101 (all) Robb Kendrick/National Geographic Image
Collection, 102 Frans Lanting/National Geographic Image Collection,
103 Peter Kaminsky/Flickr, 104, 185 (r) Frans Lanting/National
Geographic Image Collection, 105 Bobby Model, National Geographic
Image Collection, 107–108 (all) Michael S. Yamashita/National
Geographic Image Collection, 110 Jonathan Blair/National Geographic
Image Collection, 112 (t) Bobby Model/National Geographic Image
Collection, (b) Martin Gray/National Geographic Image Collection,
113 (t, b) James L. Stanfield/National Geographic Image Collection,
(c) Burt Silverman/National Geographic Image Collection, 115 (b) James
L. Stanfield/National Geographic Image Collection, 116, 186 Associated
Press, 117 W. E. Garrett/National Geographic Image Collection,
118–119 (all except globe) Robb Kendrick/National Geographic Image
Collection, 120 (t, c) Robb Kendrick/National Geographic Image
Collection, (b) Paul Chesley/National Geographic Image Collection,
122 Cristina Ciochina/Shutterstock, 123 (t, l) John Scofield/National
Geographic Image Collection, (t, r) Jodi Cobb/National Geographic Image
Collection, (b, l) George F. Mobley/National Geographic Image Collection,
124 (t) C. Beckwith & A. Fisher/National Geographic Image Collection,
(b) Randy Olson/National Geographic Image Collection, 125 (t) C. Beckwith
& A. Fisher/National Geographic Image Collection, (b, r) George
Steinmetz/National Geographic Image Collection, (b, l) Peter Carsten/
National Geographic Image Collection, 127 Karen Kasmauski/National
Geographic Image Collection, 128, 187 (t) Winfield Parks/National
Geographic Image Collection, 129, 131 (t) James L. Stanfield/National
Geographic Image Collection, 130–131 (bg) Sarah Leen/National
Geographic Image Collection, 130 Sarah Leen/National Geographic Image
Collection, 131 (b) James P. Blair/National Geographic Image Collection,
132–133 (t from l) Mark Wragg/iStockPhoto, CostinT/iStockPhoto,
Katiko/iStockPhoto, Eric Delmar/iStockPhoto, Elena Schweitzer/
iStockPhoto, Mark Evans/iStockPhoto, Gabor Izso/iStockPhoto,

132 (b, l) sweetym/iStockPhoto, (b, r) Elena Schweitzer/iStockPhoto,
134 (t, r) Gabor Izso/iStockPhoto, (t, l) Mark Wragg/iStockPhoto,
135 James Balog/National Geographic Image Collection, 137 (t) Paul
Nicklen/National Geographic Image Collection, (c, b) James Balog/National
Geographic Image Collection, 138 (l from t) Norbert Rosing/National
Geographic Image Collection, 140 (t) 20th Century Fox/The Kobal
Collection, (b) Colin Monteath/Minden Pictures/National Geographic Image
Collection, 141 (r) Nick Norman/National Geographic Image Collection,
142–143 (all) David McLain/National Geographic Image Collection,
145 Ralph Lee Hopkins/National Geographic Image Collection,
147 Michael and Patricia Fogden/Minden Pictures/National Geographic
Image Collection, 149–150 (all) Mark W. Moffett/National Geographic
Image Collection, 152 Mark Moffett/Minden Pictures/National Geographic
Images, 153 (r) James Forte/National Geographic Image Collection, (t, l)
Tim Fitzharris/Minden Pictures/National Geographic Image Collection, (b, l)
Piotr Naskrecki/Minden Pictures/National Geographic Image Collection,
154 (t) Tim Laman/National Geographic Image Collection, (b) Ira Block/
National Geographic Image Collection, 155 (all) Ira Block/National
Geographic Image Collection, 156 John Pitcher/iStockPhoto, 157 Darlyne
A. Murawski/National Geographic Image Collection, 158, 189 (t, r)
Darlyne A. Murawski/National Geographic Image Collection, (c, b) Michael
Durham/Minden Picture/National Geographic Image Collection, 159 Joe
McNally/Sygma/National Geographic Image Collection, 161 (all) James A.
Sugar/National Geographic Image Collection, 162 (b) Virgin Galactic,
164 James A. Sugar/National Geographic Image Collection, 165 (t, r)
Tim Laman/National Geographic Image Collection, (t, l) Stephen Alvarez/
National Geographic Image Collection, (b) Sisse Brimberg/National
Geographic Image Collection, 166 (all) Stephen Alvarez/National
Geographic Image Collection, 167 (t, l) Stephen Alvarez/National
Geographic Image Collection, 169 (r) Stephen Alvarez/National Geographic
Image Collection, 170, 190 (t) Stephen Alvarez/National Geographic Image
Collection, 171, 172 John Burcham/National Geographic Image Collection,
172–173 (bg) Tim Fitzharris/Minden Pictures/National Geographic Image
Collection, 173 (l) Bill Hatcher/National Geographic Image Collection,
(b) David Edwards/National Geographic Image Collection, 174 (t from l),
acilo/iStockPhoto, Clint Spencer/iStockPhoto, Matjaz Boncina/iStockPhoto,
apomares/iStockPhoto, rackermann/iStockPhoto, 176 (t from l) Matjaz
Boncina/iStockPhoto, Clint Spencer/iStockPhoto, apomares/iStockPhoto

Illustration Credits

10, 11 (b), 15 (t, l), 19 (l), 20 (b), 24 (b), 34 (l; c, l), 38 (b), 44 (b),
46 (t, l), 48–49 (c), 48 (b), 49 (b), 52 (r), 53 (c), 57 (b, l), 62 (b), 65 (b),
68 (t, l), 69 (c), 74 (b), 76, 83 (b), 86 (b), 88 (t, l), 90–91 (c), 91 (t, b),
95 (b), 96 (c), 104 (l), 106, 115 (t), 116 (t), 118 (c), 128 (b), 130 (t, l),
132–133 (bg), (c, l), (c, r), (b, r), 136, 138 (r), 141 (l), 148 (l), 158 (l),
160, 167 (r), 169 (l), 170 (b), 172 (t, l), 174–175 (c), 174 (b),
175 (c, l) National Geographic Maps, 40 (t) Kazuhiko Sano/National
Geographic Image Collection, 41 (b) John A. Bonner/National Geographic
Image Collection, 43 Gregory A. Harlin/National Geographic Image
Collection, 45 Louis S. Glanzman/National Geographic Image Collection,
46 (b, r) William H. Bond/National Geographic Image Collection,
47 (t, l) Louis S. Glanzman/National Geographic Image Collection,
52 (l) Javier Zarracina, 66 (b) NOAA National Hurricane Center/National
Geographic Image Collection, 111 Burt Silverman/National Geographic
Image Collection, 146, 188 Mark Seidler/National Geographic Image
Collection, 148 (r) John Dawson/National Geographic Image Collection,
162 (t) Virgin Galactic

Text Credits

11 Adapted from "Olive Oil—Elixir of the Gods," by Erla Zwingle:
National Geographic Magazine, Sep 1999, 16 Adapted from "True Colors:
Divided Loyalties in Puerto Rico," Online: http://ngm.nationalgeographic.
com/ngm/0303/feature2/index.html, Mar 2003, 23 Adapted from "What
Are They Doing Down There?" and "Listening to Humpbacks," by Douglas

Chadwick: National Geographic Magazine, Jan 2007/Jul 1999, 28 Adapted
from "Wolf to Woof," by Karen Lange: National Geographic Magazine,
Jan 2002, 35 Adapted from "Was King Tut Murdered?" by A. R. Williams:
National Geographic Magazine, Jun 2005, 40 Adapted from "Last Hours
of the Ice Man," by Stephen S. Hall: National Geographic Magazine, Jul
2007, 53 Adapted from "Grand Central Passion," by Susan Orlean: National
Geographic Magazine, Dec 2005, 58 Adapted from "Wonders of the West,"
by Donovan Webster: National Geographic Traveler, Nov–Dec 2006,
65 Adapted from "The Perils of New Orleans," by Joel K. Bourne, Jr. :
National Geographic Magazine, Aug 2007, 70 Adapted from "Super Storms:
No End in Sight," by Thomas Hayden: National Geographic Magazine,
Aug 2006, 77 Adapted from "Coral Reef Color," by Les Kaufman: National
Geographic Magazine, May 2005, and "Coral in Peril," by Douglas
Chadwick: National Geographic Magazine, Jan 1999, 82 Adapted from
"Great White Deep Trouble," by Peter Benchley: National Geographic
Magazine, Apr 2000, 95 Adapted from "Flower Trade," by Vivienne Walt:
National Geographic Magazine, Apr 2001, 100 Adapted from "Perfume:
The Essence of Illusion," by Cathy Newman: National Geographic
Magazine, Oct 1998, 107 Adapted from "The Adventures of Marco
Polo," by Mike Edwards: National Geographic Magazine, May–Jul 2001,
112 Adapted from "Ibn Battuta: Prince of Travelers," by Thomas J.
Abercrombie: National Geographic Magazine, Dec 1991, 119 Adapted
from "Sumo," by T. R. Reid: National Geographic Magazine, Jul 1997,
124 Adapted from "Brides of the Sahara," by Carol Beckwith: National
Geographic Magazine, Feb 1998, 137 Adapted from "The Big Thaw," by
Tim Appenzeller: National Geographic Magazine, Jun 2007, 142 Adapted
from "Last Days of the Ice Hunters," by Gretel Ehrlich: National Geographic
Magazine, Jan 2006, 149 Adapted from "Army Ants," by Edward O. Wilson:
National Geographic Magazine, Aug 2006, 154 Adapted from "Uncommon
Vision," by Lynne Warren: National Geographic Magazine, May 2002,
161 Adapted from "Rocket for the Rest of Us," by Burt Rutan: National
Geographic Magazine, Apr 2005, 166 Adapted from "Call of the Abyss,"
by Alexander Klimchouk: National Geographic Magazine, May 2005